5.51 USA
6.62 CAN
7.28 EUR

THE SNUFF TAKER'S EPHEMERIS

DEVOE'S EXTRA QUALITY COSTS YOU LESS TO USE, BECAUSE ITS QUALITY MAKES IT LAST SO LONG. *JUDGE FOR YOURSELF.* DEVOE SNUFF COMPANY, NASHVILLE, TENN.

Premiere Issue

VOLUME ONE
FALL 2010

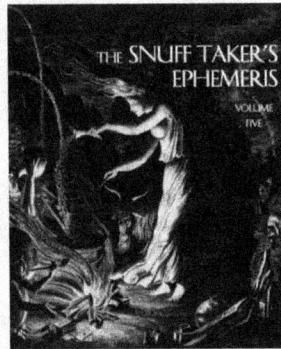  
 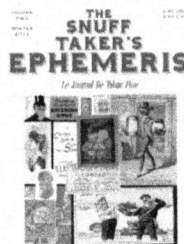  

THE SNUFF TAKER'S EPHEMERIS

VOLUME ONE

MASTER EDITION SERIES

Table of Contents

THE SNUFF TAKERS EPHEMERIS

The only publication on Earth devoted to the world's finest tobacco

5.67 us
6.22 can

PREMIERE ISSUE

PREFACE TO THE MASTER EDITION

Rob Hubbard

Whenever I'm asked questions about this magazine, it's usually one of the following three:

1. What's an efermenus? (Or, How do you pronounce efermenus?)
2. What is snuff? (Or, What is snuss?)
3. What possessed you originally to do a magazine about tobacco?

I've gotten pretty used to answering them all. Ephemeris is synonymous with "atlas" or "gazette" or "almanac", basically a collection of trivial information you would find on your grandmother's kitchen table. Rarely used today in the above context, it is still a common word that occasionally crops up in modern mathematics or astrology, usually in reference to collections of tables and charts of data. And it's pronounced a myriad of ways:

1. EFF-uhh-MEER-us
2. EFFIM-ur-us
3. Ef- EEM-ur-us

I personally pronounce it option #1, but many seem to prefer option #2. College professors and bearded intellectuals go for option #3. Oh, and guess what the plural form of Ephemeris is: *Ephemerides*. I love calling a printer up and saying "have you got my stack of ephemerides ready?" I once had a woman tell her boss that I was calling her and asking for amphetamines.

The second question is usually answered by me giving the interested party my card and telling them to order a copy of the book if they want to find out what snus and snuff are. I've long since stopped trying to explain the difference between the snuff that Napoleon inhaled versus the snuff your daddy dipped. I don't even correct people who call it "snuss." (If you're a first time reader- you are forgiven. Snus rhymes with "moose" and "caboose," which is exactly the part of the body I want to kick when an all-knowing tobagophile makes an ass of himself by mispronouncing a one-syllable, four-letter word.)

The third question I've answered on occasion, and I believe I've written articles or done interviews in which I pretty much went into all the details behind the formation of the STE, but I'll share that story here, hopefully, for the last time. Though the roots of the Ephemeris go back to me reading Tom Dunn's *Pipe Smoker's Ephemeris* while growing up, the actual conception began in May 2010. I was on my way to the dentist for an extraction and I realized I was almost a half an hour early for my appointment. I decided to kill some time at the bookstore across the street and went up and down the newsstand looking for something that caught my eye.

Down in the corner, in the back next to the marijuana magazines, was *Cigar Aficionado* and *Cigar Press*. Even though smokeless is my favorite, I'm not one to turn down a nice cigar or pipe. I like reading about smoking almost as much as I like the actual ritual, so I flipped through the two books and was astonished to see how badly *Aficionado* had deteriorated in the last ten years or so since I picked up a copy. Sure, there was lots of color ads for cigar brands that two years later aren't even on the market anymore. Sure, there was an interview with the crew of *Entourage*, which I don't watch and wondered what it was doing in a cigar mag (turns out one of the cast members occasionally smoked cigars). Sure, there was articles about golfing and Rolex watches and ink pens and resort getaways in Tahiti... but where was the **tobacco?** (The other magazine was a little more grounded in cigar coverage so I picked it up and ended up being disappointed anyway. I left it in the lobby of the dentist's office.)

While the pleasant waves of euphoric nitrous oxide propelled me to cloud nine, I had a vision. A *real* tobacco magazine. A magazine for folks that cared more about how Burley was grown than how to hail a cab in Argentina. A book with articles about the history and current use of tobacco. We would shy away from cigars (because there's already about 15 such magazines on the market today) and cigarettes (because we all felt they suck and had successfully kicked our addictions to them) and focus on only the finest tobacco, which in my mind is nasal snuff and Swedish-style snus. Pipe tobacco should be featured occasionally, along with good old chewing quids. Hell, we could even cover such arcane nicotiana as Fuomo Loco and Devil's Snuff, and other hallucinogenic strains that they don't tell you about in *Cigar Press*. It would be a celebration of all things tobacco: a magazine I felt hadn't existed since Tom Dunn's legendary *Pipe Smoker's Ephemeris* ceased publication.

Then the anesthesia began to wear off and I screamed as the dentist's scalpel pierced the nerve cluster surrounding my sixth wisdom tooth extraction of the day. (Yes, I said sixth- for some reason I'll never understand, God gifted me with eight impacted wisdom teeth. I've still got two more to pull...)

I kicked the idea around all night. I called around for estimates and found that I could finance the publication of one issue. If the book made any money, or we lined up enough advertisers, we could do a second issue. I took the down payment I was saving on a new Smartcar and set it aside for this "project," as my wife dubbed it.

I called Mick Hellwig up and offered him the title of Editor-in-Chief. "What would my job be?" he asked. "To deal with the people, since I'm socially retarded," I answered. "Sounds good," he said, and a partnership was born. Micah Rimel, my oldest friend, didn't "officially" come on board until the second issue, but I had him in mind for Managing Editor since day one.

I've been a writer for several years, and I knew I could come up with at least half of the material for the project, but I would need other authors to round out the stable. I contacted folks like Simon Handelsman, possibly the world's foremost authority on snuffboxes, and he agreed to pen an ongoing column. Anthony Haddad, also known as Dr. Snus, was another writer friend that frequented the same snus circles online, and he gladly jumped on board. There was David Thigpen, a writer that had served as an interim editor at *Fortean Times* and had a wealth of knowledge about bizarre accidents and weird facts about nearly every subject imaginable. I told him to dig up what trivia he could find about tobacco and we'd pen an article around it.

Other writers found out about the project and contacted me personally. They had some great ideas and I invited them along. Even though no one was being paid for their work, they didn't care. The fact that they were going to be able to write about their favorite subject and actually have it published was payment enough (thank goodness). The same can be said of all of the artists, designers and friends and family that did things like call half of the tobacco stores in the US and attempt to get them to pre-order this new magazine. It was a communal project that everyone was psyched about. Everyone except the tobacco companies; we couldn't convince a single one to purchase ad space for the issue. (That would change with Volume II). And after a few months, we had enough material to go to print.

I'm not going to get into the horrid nightmare of getting the first edition published; that was covered in the introduction to the Second Edition. This **Master Edition** is the fifth and final printing. The previous editions came out like this (collectors take note):

1. The first printing was limited to 100 copies distributed to staff members. It was in really bad shape and I was ashamed to even give them away.

2. The second printing, done a couple of days later, consisted of 1000 copies to distribute to the paying customers and potential advertisers. My wife and I spent three days pulling the staples out of the center of the book and flipping some of the interior pages around since they had been printed upside down. We then manually re-stapled the spine and sent them off. Some of these were signed and numbered, but I can't remember how many.

3. The third printing of 5000 copies was shipped out to stores across the country. These were basically the same as the second printing, but instead of upside down pages, they had miscut edges that trimmed off several lines of text throughout the book. Amazingly, they went on to completely sell out.

*4. In June 2011, **Volume One Redux** was released. It was basically a cleaned up, squarebound copy that aesthetically matched our printing of Volume II. This batch consisted of 2500 copies. The first 500 off the line were signed and numbered.*

That brings us to the edition that you now hold in your hands. With our Fifth Volume, we drastically changed the size of the magazine to its current 8x10 format, dwarfing the previous digest-sized issues. We also began to sell out of our back stock, leaving new readers unable to purchase printed editions of our early issues. (Now, as always, we offer the Digital E-dition as a portable, convenient, full color and eco/wallet-friendly substitute to our print copy.) But there are many folks, myself included, who insist on the printed page.

We decided to reprint our first four issues in their entirety in the new format. This would help new readers round out their collection as well as giving old readers the option to read their favorite articles in a font size that doesn't induce blindness. But we'd also throw in extras, like commentary and concept work that never saw the light of day. Sort of a "director's cut," if you will.

Beginning with Volume One, this **Master Edition** series will reprint the first four issues of *The Snuff Taker's Ephemeris*, complete and unabridged, warts and all, mistakes intact. Look for the next three installments to come out during 2013.

Throughout this edition, you'll find annotations from me regarding the stories behind the articles. If you're not interested in reading such recollections, you have my blessing to skip these sections entirely. The "magic" in these pages come from the original material- not from our footnotes and additions. Thank you for your support the last few years; we can't do it without you.

-RW Hubbard
President & Publisher

FOREWORD

MICK HELLWIG

Upon receiving my first printing of the first issue of the STE I was blown away. Here in my hands was the culmination of months of planning, talking, writing, hoping, wishing, effort and frustration. It was a lot of work, but in that moment I knew it was a bargain at double the problems and effort to us.

When I was a young teenager I had a dream of being a writer (actually I dreamed of being a Famous Author, but whatever.) My first attempt at a short story was great in my mind. My father disagreed and took an odd pleasure in pointing out all my factual mistakes. Well, Dad didn't know anything so I approached my English teacher, who happened to be a distant cousin, who pointed out all the grammatical errors and remarked that I would never be a Hemingway. Thus ended my blossoming career as a fiction writer. But the dream never really left me. Many years later I began to write a bit on SnusCentral.org and the bug bit me again. I still will never be a Hemingway, but at least I get to write. STE gives me the chance to write a little but it gives me two things that, to my more mature mind, matter more.

I gives me a chance to grant other aspiring writers a forum to get their work in print. We didn't (and don't) ask for perfection, we only ask for passion. A passion for tobacco, or fiction stories that sort of involve tobacco, or just a *good* story. Most of the writers you read in our pages second guess their talent. The owners have never lied to a one of them, we like everything we have printed. As far as I know we have never even sent a single article back to them asking it to be reworked. Sure, we need to correct spelling and maybe grammar [**Look who's talking!- RWH**] but that is expected in any magazine. In this reprint I would again like to publicly thank each and every person who has written an article or story for our magazine. You guys and gals truly are what makes us look good.

Second; STE is a tangible accomplishment that I can hold in my hands. I've made a mark on the world. It may be a small mark in a small section of the world, but 50 years from now my grandchildren can hold that same copy of our first issue and be amazed that Gramps was involved in printing a magazine. Heck, my 17 year old daughter is amazed her dad is involved in a magazine.

I've had several jobs in my lifetime, none of which has any real lasting effect beyond a few days. I don't build things. I can't point to a building and say I put the bricks in that wall. With the STE I can point to something and say "that's me". Tom Dunn, the inspiration for our magazine and its name, made a much bigger impact than I suspect he even imagined. No, I don't have delusions of grandeur. I understand we are fighting an uphill battle to even break through the background noise in the world of print media, and the chances of us successfully making it to the top shelf at every bookstore in America are very small. Even if we fail, we can at least show we tried. There are a lot of copies of STE out there in the world. We have a great fan base and a great team assembled to keep bringing our fans more of what has turned out to be a labor of love that isn't really that much of a labor. Sure, it's tough to keep the momentum going at times, but it is not "work" in the usual sense. This type of work is not a dirty four letter word.

We started STE to be something Rob and I would want to read and we were arrogant enough to believe that others would want to read it also. Thank you for justifying our faith in ourselves. Thank you for continuing to read and purchase STE. We plan to keep on producing it the best way we can. With the help of our friends, readership and contributors we really can't lose.

Mick Hellwig

VOLUME

ONE

FALL
2010

8.83 USA

9.99 CAN

THE
SNUFF
TAKER'S
EPHEMERIS

Tidskriften av snus och snuff

DEVOE'S

PURE SNUFF

EXTRA QUALITY
EAGLE MILLS
SCOTCH SNUFF

DEVOE'S EXTRA QUALITY COSTS
YOU LESS TO USE, BECAUSE ITS
QUALITY MAKES IT LAST SO LONG.
JUDGE FOR YOURSELF.
DEVOE SNUFF COMPANY, NASHVILLE, TENN.

Premiere Issue

COLLECTOR'S EDITION

THIS ISSUE IS DEDICATED TO

LARRY WATERS

WITHOUT WHOM
NONE OF THIS
WOULD HAVE
BEEN
POSSIBLE.

-H & H

First Master Edition printing: November 2012.

ISBN 10: 0985478128

ISBN 13: 978-0-9854781-2-4

On the cover: DeVoe's Eagle Mills Snuff

TUMBLERS ARE VALUABLE
BOTTLES ARE WASTED MONEY

DeVoe's Eagle Mills Snuff was chosen to adorn our inaugural issue because it's truly an international product that has, at one time, represented all major styles of snuff.

The Eagle Mills were built in Spottswood, NJ by French Huguenot Isaac DeVoe (nee, *Deveaux*) somewhere around 1835. Isaac began by milling popular brands of French snuff of the time, such as Paris *Rapé* (later, *Rappee*) and Carrotte *Parfume*.

While the brands initially sold well, in order to penetrate the lucrative Midwestern snuff market, DeVoe hired mill hands from all over the world to make regional snuffs. Soon he had Scots-Irish, Scandinavian, Bavarian and Polish snuffmakers turning out recipes for dozens of different DeVoe brands.

In addition to the French blends, there was Lundy Foot (also sold as Irish High Toast and Irish Blackguard), Plain Scotch, Sweet Scotch, Rose Maccoboy (also sold as Polish and Holland snuff), Eagle Snus (also sold as Salted Scotch, Swedish, and Eagle Mills [Swedish] Chewing Snuff), German; and all of the other major styles of the era: SP, Medicated, Brunswick (Black Rappee), Burgundy and Göteborg Rappee.

Around the turn of the century, DeVoe (like pretty much every single tobacco maker in the country) found itself under the umbrella of the American Tobacco Company, which later devolved into the American Snuff Company. In 1911, after the American trust was dissolved, DeVoe was taken by Weyman-Bruton (makers of Copenhagen and Bruton Snuff). In 1922, Weyman-Bruton became the United States Tobacco Company.

Today, the only remainder of the DeVoe snuff legacy is DeVoe Sweet Snuff, which can still be found on some store shelves, although Altria has officially de-listed it from their product catalog. It remains to be seen if the DeVoe brand has truly met its fate...

STE

9

STAFF

R.W. HUBBARD
PRESIDENT AND PUBLISHER

MICK HELLWIG
EDITOR-IN-CHIEF

MICAH RIMEL
MANAGING EDITOR

WRITING STAFF:

JENNIFER GOLDSMITH

ANTHONY HADDAD

PAT HAGER

SIMON HANDELSMAN

MICK HELLWIG

RW HUBBARD

BILL JOHNSON

MICAH RIMEL

DAVID THIGPEN

JAMES WALTER

LARRY WATERS

CONTENTS

VOLUME ONE
FALL 2010

COMMENTARY

IN EACH ISSUE

THE SNUFF TAKER'S EPHEMERIS IS PUBLISHED SIX TIMES A YEAR BY LUCIEN PUBLISHING,
FAYETTEVILLE NC. VOLUME ONE, DECEMBER 2010. COST IS 8.83 (USA) FOR A SINGLE
ISSUE, 35.32 PER YEAR. ADDRESS: PO BOX 287, SPRING LAKE, NC 28390. WWW:
SNUFFMAGAZINE.ORG AND STEPHEMERIS.COM. ADVERTISING AND DISTRIBUTION / BULK
PURCHASE ORDER QUERIES: DISTRIBUTION@STEPHEMERIS.COM. THE SNUFF TAKER'S
EPHEMERIS IS PROUDLY PRINTED IN THE USA ON 100% ARCHIVAL GRADE, ACID-FREE VIRGIN
PAPER STOCK. FIRST PRINTING, OCTOBER 2010. SECOND PRINTING, MAY 2011.

Introduction to the Second Printing

Well, where to begin?

What you're holding in your hands is the culmination of almost a year's worth of work. Initially, Mick and I thought the hard part would be putting a magazine together for the first time. Hell, that was pretty simple. The difficult thing was getting the damned thing published.

I guess technically, this edition should be considered the *fourth* printing instead of the second. The first printer that I used screwed the book up so badly that I refused the order. I kept about 100 copies from this destroyed batch and divvied them up amongst friends and staff members.

In a rush to locate a local print house that could read and write in English, I found one that could get the book out within a few days. So I had them print up a thousand copies to send out to all the pre-order customers. This second printing was almost as bad as the first, but I had no choice but to send it out as it was. I hated to do it, but people were phoning our office wondering when their copy would arrive in the mail.

So now that the online orders were taken care of, I needed a salable product that I could ship out to our bookstores and tobacconists. I hit the internet and found a company that claimed that they could do a better job than their competitors at half the price. Let's just say that they were a little ambitious in their claims (but they did produced the nicest covers out of all three batches). Once these books shipped out, we were out of stock.

We expected that we'd get a ton of return copies from the newsstand retailers, but surprisingly they all sold out. This left us without anything to offer the 20 or 30 customers a day who were writing and calling us wanting to know where they could snag a copy of our first issue.

We knew that we'd have to reprint this issue, but we wanted to wait until we found a better printer. With our second issue, we found a local company who (just like us) was just starting up and wanted to make a name for itself. Volume II came out looking pretty good and the printers are wonderful people to work with. We've learned a lot from each other, and we anticipated growing together over the next several years.

But a crazy thing happened when it came time to reprint this issue. First, there was the tornadoes. They ripped through our state and completely decimated a section of downtown that just happened to house our print offices. Thankfully, no one was hurt, but our printer was left without an office.

They called me and told me that they could still get the book out in May, it would just be delayed a couple of weeks. "No problem!" I said. "This was completely beyond anyone's control and I'm sure our readers will understand."

A couple of weeks later, they called back and said that they would have the book ready by May 17th. "Excellent," I said, "but I'm going to be out of the country until May 22nd." I needed to be there to approve the final product before they could receive payment.

They assured me that they would hold the batch until I could show up in person. Meanwhile, I toured Europe with a group of guys from *The Ephemeris* as well as Snuscentral and some other online snus sites

The whole time I was there, I had my fingers crossed, hoping that this issue would look perfect and I could finally be proud enough to hand it out to my friends, family and readers and say "See! This is what it was *supposed* to look like the first time."

When I got back to the US on Monday morning, jetlagged and exhausted, I put in a call to our printer and got their voicemail. I left a message, figuring they were probably backed up with work. When they didn't call back the next day, I left another message.

Wednesday, I drove over to the shop and was surprised to see it closed. There was a hand-written sign on the window that said "Back In Two Hours." I didn't like how this was playing out, so I went and killed some time at the library and came back later that afternoon. It was still closed. Now I was pissed.

Thursday I came back and the shop was still closed. I went over to the car dealer next door and inquired about the print shop. The guy at the car dealership told me that they hadn't seen anyone there in a week.

By this time, I was both angry and worried about our magazine. Then I started thinking that maybe something had happened to the staff. Maybe they were all dead in the back room, victims of a robbery homicide? This fear was allayed when a grey Toyota pulled up next to me and I saw the owner's daughter behind the wheel. Before I could even approach her vehicle, she sped off in reverse as if I were chasing her with a battleaxe.

By the time I got home, there was a message on their website stating that they had a family emergency and were filing for Chapter 11 bankruptcy. Thankfully, I hadn't paid the printing bill in advance. (Note to aspiring self-publishers: never, ever, under any circumstance pay for your job until you hold the final product in your hands.)

So, I'm writing this on Saturday, May 28th 2011 and I'm hoping to find a printer by Tuesday and have this book out again. It seems like this issue is cursed. Like the publishing gremlin demon imp things are stalking the contents of this magazine.

Anyway, there's the story of how this reprint came to be. Hopefully what you're now holding in your hands lives up to your expectations, and we apologize for all delays that have transpired in the meantime.

Happy trails,
RW Hubbard

PS: Here's a pic of Mick (right) and I (sitting) trying to figure out how to work a 600-year old Swedish printing press in order to get this mag out on time. (We gave up when we realized it didn't recognize .pdf files.)

R.w.H./S.T.E.

LETTERS

Even though this is our first issue, we had a few letters that we decided to run. We sent out advanced copies of certain articles to reviewers and advertisers, and here is their response:

Dear Ephemeris:

Wow, I'm stunned! An entire magazine devoted to smokeless tobacco? Who'da thunk it? Although I must say that you are attempting a fool's errand by coming out with a print mag right now, what with the interwebs and all. But it certainly requires chutzpah, which you have in spades.

You mentioned Cigar Aficionado [in our last conversation]- please, please PLEASE do not model yourself after that publication. Cigar Aficionado ceased being relevant ten years ago when they gave up on tobacco and started focusing on golf. Anyway, keep up the good work.

David Smith
Winston-Salem, NC

David, The Ephemeris is the anti-Aficionado of tobacco journalism. You will never, I repeat, NEVER read an article in our book about golf, ink pens, Rolex watches or Italian leather loafers unless it somehow involves snuff or snus. Not that we have anything against the above-listed doodads, but they have no place in a tobacco-themed publication.

Yo!

I got the copy of your haunted mill article [see page 40] today. Believe it or not, I've actually been inside the George Helme mill before. My uncle was a custodian there during the eighties, and I would go up and visit him some nights when he was working. Me and my cousins would go bug him and sometimes we would steal some dip cans straight off the assembly line.

My uncle told me stories about a woman that died there one night on the assembly line, and it was supposedly her ghost that was haunting the warehouse. I never saw anything personally, but I heard a lot of stories. Even when that place was still operational, it was a pretty bleak building.

Jerry Kimetko
Trenton, New Jersey

The article on the Cedar Grove snuff mill was put together shortly before going to press, and we were lucky to have been put in touch with a Mrs. Gillian Bromley, who worked at the Wilson of Sharrow Mill some time ago. Mrs. Bromley has agreed to pen a follow-up to our article recounting her experiences in the mill, and we eagerly look forward to it!

Guys,

Glad to see a magazine about the snuff culture that is going strong today. There's magazines about every subject under the sun except for snuff, so I think that there's plenty of room for you in today's marketplace. All the best,

James Heath
Birmingham, England

And that's all for our first letter column. Send us your thoughts on this issue to **letters@STephemeris.com** *or via post at:*

LETTERS
C/O THE EPHEMERIS
PO BOX 287
SPRING LAKE, NC
28390 (USA)

See you in sixty!
-Ed.

Welcome, and thank you for purchasing the inaugural issue of *The Snuff Taker's Ephemeris*.

My name is Mick Hellwig. Some of you know me, but for the rest… I am a middle aged, lower middle-class American tobacco user. Oral snuff in high school. Several years spent smoking two packs of cigarettes per day. Currently, I use Swedish snus and nasal snuff from all over the world. I smoke an occasional pipe or cigar. I still sneak in a can of dip or pouch of loose leaf chewing tobacco a few times a year. I am fascinated by history in general and tobacco history specifically. I get jazzed when I realize I am partaking of tobacco using the same modes and methods that my ancestors used 400 years ago.

You are holding in your hand the physical manifestation of a dream. A slightly crazy man, Rob Hubbard, approached me a few months ago and suggested that we start a print magazine devoted to the history, culture and use of smokeless tobacco. My first response was "You're insane!" In this internet age, why take a step *backwards* and do a print magazine?

After discussing it for a few hours over the course of a week, his exuberance and passion won over all my objections. So it began.

We have assembled a great core group of knowledgeable contributors. From people who have been in the tobacco business longer than most of our readers have been alive, to guys who are so new they still remember the date of their first snus order. We even have one person who doesn't use tobacco at all (but since he knows his history so well, we let that slide…)

We are sticking to an old-fashioned print form for a few reasons, the main one being that Rob and I *are* a couple of old fashioned guys that tend to think the old ways are best, sometimes.

Another reason is that while the internet is great, there are times when nothing will satisfy quite like holding a book in your hand. As my wife says, "It's kind of dangerous to have your laptop in the bathtub." Yeah…

But perhaps most importantly, for me, is that the information contained in these pages is truly timeless. Books like Bryan Bergeron's *Dark Ages II* and Nicholson Baker's *Double Fold* illustrate just how useless digital media is for historical preservation. Since the 4th Millennium BC, the written page has yet to be superceded as a means of archival recordkeeping, and it likely never will.

A large part of what we have to share is reprinted from old books, magazines and newspapers. It just seems right to put these items back into print. Some of what we will show you only existed, until now, in the memories of those that have lived it, or heard the stories from their families.

Many months ago Rob told me a few stories from his personal family history in the tobacco business. I told him he should write those stories down. My advice for you, dear reader, is the same. If you have stories of tobacco in your memory, write them down, send them to us. If we like what you have written, we will get them in print, as space and time permits. The Ephemeris is not just us, or our core group, it is all of you. There are many pieces of this puzzle and we, honestly, need all the help we can get putting it together.

I hope you enjoy the magazine as much as we are enjoying bringing it to you. Feel free to contact Rob or myself with any suggestions, comments or questions.

-MICK HELLWIG

I wish I could say that this magazine is a culmination of years of hard work and careful planning, but I would be lying.

The genesis of the book has already been printed elsewhere, so here's the condensed version: I wanted a tobacco-themed magazine to read at the dentist's office, and the cigar magazines were looking pretty weak. Then it hit me- why not do my *own* tobacco magazine, and make it just as prestigious as *Cigar Aficionado*, but point the focus squarely on smokeless tobacco? Six months later, here we are.

I wanted to shake everyone's perception of what a snuff taker is. Pipe smokers are portrayed as intellectuals or eccentric old men. Cigar smokers are successful businessmen. Cigarette smokers are white trash, followed by the *lowest scum on earth*, smokeless tobacco users. Only the mullet-headed trailer park resident with the '87 Camaro up on blocks uses smokeless tobacco.

Except that's not true. Most cigar smokers I know are poseurs that want to *seem* successful or to look cool. You could replace the label on a Philly Blunt with that of a Cuban *Montecristo* and the dumb SOB's wouldn't notice the difference.

Not all cigarette smokers are horrible people. Here in North Carolina, just about everyone smokes or has smoked cigarettes. Trying to make a generalization would be stupid, as the people that buy cigarettes come from all walks of life. To paint all of them as low-class subhumans would reveal one's own ignorance.

While it's true that many of my fellow pipe smokers can be classed into the three main stereotypes (intellectual, eccentric or old), just as many are dumb as bricks or young and conformist. In fact, most people that I know that smoke pipes aren't smoking *tobacco* at all!

In most parts of the United States, when one hears the word "snuff tobacco," they instantly picture a can of Copenhagen or Skoal along with a cowboy or Nascar driver spitting a long stream of brown mucus into the wind. And while many snuff takers use oral snuff, and while many oral snuff users do fit the stereotype, there exists more exceptions to the rule than many care to admit.

There is the Scandinavian snus taker. Snus, an evolution of nasal snuff originating in Sweden in the early 1800's, is used by millions of Nordic men and women from all walks of life. Ingvar Kamprad, founder of IKEA and one of the richest men in the world, is a snus taker. Snus is as common in Scandinavia as cigarettes are everywhere else.

In America, it was two Danish snuff mill workers that shared their snus recipe with George Weyman, resulting in Copenhagen Snuff, which has been a perennial favorite since 1822. The preacher, the politician, the lawyer and the doctor all "dip" snuff, no matter what the bourgeois would have you believe.

Then there is the nasal snuffer. Though not as popular in the US as it is in Europe, there is a renaissance of new snuffers eager to explore the method of consumption that reigned supreme over smoking for centuries. There are those that wish to give up the more harmful effects of cigarettes by switching to the relatively risk-free world of snuff and snus.

Whatever the attraction, snuffers are not stupid, poor, ignorant or unhealthy. Snuffers are a varied and determined lot. They don't care what others think about them, and they are quick to tell you exactly where you can stick your stereotype. And *this* is their magazine.

-RW Hubbard

Annotations, Footnotes, Skewed Memories and Other Trivial Facts Regarding The Making of The Snuff Taker's Ephemeris Volume One

as Recounted By RW Hubbard

The cover to the first printing was thrown together at the last minute. I scanned an old DeVoe calendar book and cleaned it up digitally before writing the accompanying text ("On the Cover.") DeVoe was chosen to represent the magazine because the company had at one time or another experimented with all styles of snuff, including snus. The strange cover price ($5.52 US/$6.61 Canada) was Mick's idea. "Why does everything you buy end in .99?" he asked. "Let's end in a weird number, like .66 or .67." I thought it was a great idea. Even when we had to raise the price, we went to 8.82 instead of 8.99. When I tried to explain this to our new distributor, they thought we were crazy. So that's why our current cover price is $10.99.

****

The first issue was saddle stitched (two staples down the seam) but it made the book look bulky towards the spine. When we did the second issue, we pretty much knew we were moving to a squarebound format, which we also utilized for the reprinting of Volume One (known in-house as *STE Volume One Redux*). Some of the formatting had to be rearranged but the *Redux* featured the same content as the first printing, with a new bonus intro from me. The cover was slightly altered, too. The STE logo and cover image stood out on a stark white background instead of the original parchment style of the first printing. We honestly couldn't afford the fancy paper the second time around and so snow-white non-laminate cardstock became the order of the day. (We used the same stock on Volume II as well).

****

Word had spread early in some circles that we were doing a new snuff magazine, which is how we ended up with a short letter column for our first issue (along with the letter that prompted the Haunted Snuff Mill story, which I received through the Snuscentral website.) We didn't really know how to respond except for "OK, thanks," which is pretty funny compared to the longwinded and detailed responses letter-writers are used to getting from us nowadays.

****

The Editorials from Mick and I were thrown together the day before we went to press. Again, I didn't really have anything deep to say, so I basically paraphrased part of an article I wrote for Snuscentral while Mick recounted my attempts at trying to get him to do a magazine with me.

****

CONTINUED ON PAGE 30

EPHEMERA

Zuka Black called "nose candy" by sensationalist *Sun* Reporter

Anti-smoking campaigners have slammed a new snuff product, claiming that it is unsafe and is being targeted at teenagers.

The tobacco product, Zuka Black, is inhaled through the nose that gives the user a nicotine hit.

It was introduced in the UK markets last month and has already sold more than 100,000, but has been condemned by Drugscope and Ash.

Amanda Sandford from Ash said that the product is certainly not safe as it contains tobacco and is being marketed towards the teenagers.

"There is no such thing as a safe tobacco product. This is clearly being targeted at young people - it does contain tobacco and people can get cancer from it, The Sun quoted her, as saying.

Zuka is packaged in a fag-packet-sized box **[No, not *that* kind of fag, the British kind. –Ed.]** that when opened, splits across the middle. It contains a cotton handkerchief and a bullet shaped dispenser inside which can be loaded and sniffed

from. It contains 60 hits of tobacco that is equivalent to 20 cigarettes.

"Snuff is neither safe nor glamorous and indeed can be pretty disgusting," said Martin Barnes, Chief Executive of Drugscope.

However, Zuka was defended by Philip Ashby Rudd, Managing Director of Zuka, who said that the product provided tobacco in a socially acceptable way to the people.

"The country has gone cold turkey overnight. At least this way those smokers that wish to continue enjoying tobacco after the ban can get their nicotine in a socially acceptable way that doesn't require them to stand outside in the rain every time they want to satisfy a craving. This is smoke without the fire," he said.

– *The Sun*
12-15-07

Editor's note: the original headline to this piece when it ran in *The Sun* was "Nicotine Nose Candy Slammed." An accompanying photo of a man taking a sniff was labeled "Nicotine Nose Candy," as if the cocaine allusion was not clear enough the first time around.

The original author of this piece, **Lachlan Cartwright**, is better known for his celebrity muckraking than he is for his journalistic integrity, so we'll leave it at that.

REQUIEM FOR A SPUD

This year will mark the Silver Anniversary of Mr. Potatohead's historic vow to set a better example for America's children by giving up the pipe.

During the first annual *Great American Smokeout* of 1986, Mr. Potatohead ceremoniously surrendered his pipe to then-Surgeon General C. Everett Koop. "I thought I was doing the right thing," claims Mr. Potatohead. "Koop had me brainwashed into thinking I was some sort of generation spokesmodel or something."

He recalls that after the ceremony, "There was supposed to be this big afterparty. I get there, and everyone's doing blow off of a glass table. Koop and Nancy [Reagan] were off in a corner swigging Hennessy and feeling each other up, and Ronnie was too busy telling racist jokes to notice what was going on. I walk up to Ed Meese, and he's standing there with a big piece of sausage, and he's like, holding it in front of his crotch. You know, like a big dong."

(RIGHT)

MAY 15, 1972: POTATOHEAD IN HAPPIER TIMES, ATTENDING A FUNDRAISER FOR GOV. GEORGE WALLACE.

Disgusted and disillusioned by the private behavior of his colleagues, Potatohead found himself shunned by his former friends. "They wouldn't talk to me anymore. They acted like they didn't know me. All of the sudden, the networks are canceling my commercials. They canned my cartoon. The big chain stores stopped carrying my toys. I had been blacklisted, and I was flat broke."

Potatohead began his three decade-long descent into obscurity and drug addiction soon after the silent boycott. "Without tobacco, I had no outlet anymore," he recalls, "No release. I began beating on Mrs. Potatohead and I got locked up a few times for domestic battery. When I was in jail, I started doing dope. Crack cocaine had just come out, and I was like 'Hey, I wonder if Koop still has my old pipe!'[laughs]."

Other charges would follow, ranging from simple possession to prostitution and manslaughter. "I had hit rock bottom. I no longer had any friends. I decided to start over. I switched to snus. Now I can get the nicotine my body needs without having to answer to the Anti-tobacco zealots. They don't even know I have it in my lip."

We at the **Ephemeris** wish Mr. Potatohead continued success with his sobriety.

Sheik Omar issues perfunctory Fatwa

June 28, 2010 - The Supreme Council of Darul Ifta of the Philippines in Cotabato City, headed by Grand Mufti Sheikh Omar Pasigan, unanimously ruled and released an Islamic Ruling or (*Fatwa*) that states using tobacco is considered "haram" or forbidden. This means that no Muslim may manufacture, buy, sell, trade or promote tobacco since these actions represent "aiding someone in committing a sin."

The Department of Health and the growing number of anti-tobacco advocates hail the Fatwa and believe that this declaration would persuade many to quit immediately and would carry anti-tobacco messages to their communities. "There is no single benefit one can derive from smoking," Health Secretary Esperanza Cabral said, adding that quitting greatly reduces health risks and produces immediate and long-term health benefits.

In 2002, the two holy cities of Mecca and Medina in Saudi Arabia were declared tobacco-free. All commercial activities involving tobacco are prohibited within the boundaries of the two cities. No form of tobacco advertising is permitted around the holy zones.

"Let us all join hands with our Muslim brothers toward a 100% tobacco-free Philippines," Cabral concluded.

- ORIGINALLY REPORTED BY THE A.P.

When told that they would no longer be able to sell tobacco products, 40 million Muslim shopkeepers worldwide all shrugged their shoulders in unison and continued selling tobacco products.

FDA Struggles To regulate E-cigs

Sept. 9, 2010-

In yet another glowing example of pompous arrogance, the Food and Drug Administration sent five E-Cig manufacturers a cease-and-desist letter today stating that they were violating federal law by manufacturing devices that contain nicotine.

The five US-based companies represent just a few of the estimated eight hundred E-Cig companies worldwide.

One of the companies singled out, Ruyan America, hasn't even manufactured E-Cigs in over a year. The letter came as a surprise to Ruyan's Willam Bartkowski, who said "I suppose the FDA didn't get the memo."

While the FDA has no real authority to regulate such products, most manufacturers lack the funds to fight a lengthy court battle. What happens next remains to be seen.

But... think of the children!

An effort to extinguish New York city's ban on flavored chewing tobacco is up in smoke.

The maker of Skoal and Copenhagen smokeless tobacco sued the city claiming only the feds can regulate the sale of tobacco products.

Manhattan Federal Judge Colleen McMahon shot them down Wednesday, saying federal law allows communities to set their own policies about access to tobacco.

"This decision ... is not only a win for us, but for the children of New York City," said City Council Speaker Christine Quinn.

"Our law is a good progressive law that will protect our youngest New Yorkers. If tobacco companies think they can fight common-sense legislation, this court decision clearly shows otherwise."

The 2009 law bars the sale of flavored cigars and chewing tobacco except in tobacco bars.

It does not cover flavored cigarettes or menthol chewing tobacco but focuses on flavors favored by teens - vanilla, chocolate, honey, candy, fruit-flavored and spices.

-Alison Gendar, *Daily News*

Snuff: a Tradition That Still Persists

By Erica Brown

(Reprinted from the *New York Times* , March 23, 1983)

LONDON, March 22— Taking snuff was the epitome of elegance 150 years ago, complete with its own social ritual. In modern times it has been associated with eccentric minorities such as dons and maiden aunts. But now it looks as if it may enjoy new popularity - for health reasons.

In recent tests at the addiction research unit of Maudsley Hospital here, half a dozen volunteers were asked to use nasal drops made of liquid snuff instead of smoking cigarettes.

"Since it's made from tobacco, snuff contains nicotine just like a cigarette," explained Dr. M.A.H. Russell, who was in charge of the project. "Although nicotine is addictive, it is not that which makes smoking so dangerous. It is the inhalation of tar, which causes lung cancer and bronchitis, and of such gases as carbon monoxide and oxides of nitrogen, which are associated with heart disease. None of these is present in snuff."

"We found that taking a small amount of the liquid snuff in each nostril gave the same nicotine buzz as one cigarette in about the same time," Dr. Russell continued. "We hope that, eventually, smokers will be able to use the drops as a substitute and then gradually wean themselves off the nicotine habit."

But why, ask the small band of snuff makers left in Britain, make life complicated? Why not just sniff snuff in its original powdered form?

"People say it's messy," commented Vivian Rose, who runs G. Smith & Sons, the last snuff specialists in London. "They associate it with dandruff and dirty fingernails. But our customers are among the most fastidious of people: lawyers, doctors, military and naval officers and a fair smattering of women. After all, with snuff you don't pollute the air, nor do you leave cigarette ash and butts in your wake."

Snuff is, basically, cured tobacco leaves ground to a fine powder. The grinding process releases the natural ammonia in

FLAVORED TOBACCO (**LEFT**) BANNED IN NEW YORK CITY. FLAVOR FLAV (**RIGHT**) STILL LEGAL, THOUGH HEAVILY REGULATED.

the leaves, which gives snuff its pungency. Almost all snuffs are also blended with floral essences, spices or menthol.

Mr. Rose buys his more than 50 blends (traditionally called sorts) of snuff from three mills in Kendal, a small market town in the Lake District. The mills are easy to locate: You just follow your nose.

'We use nine different tobaccos to get the various colors and grind to three different textures, coarse, medium and fine," said Geoffrey Gawith, managing director of Gawith Hoggarth, one of the three mills. "Then we blend in the pure essences, very much as a perfumer blends scents."

Taking snuff, along with pipe smoking, was one of the original ways of tobacco use introduced from the New World in the early 1600's. It hit its heyday during the Regency in the early 19th century, when Beau Brummell made it fashionable and the Prince Regent was a notable connoisseur, blending his own. Both men and women took snuff, and boxes of gold and silver, engraved, painted and enameled, were a minor art.

Then, as now, a few grains of snuff should be taken between forefinger and thumb, inhaled gently into the lower part of the nostril and then gradually ingested through normal breathing. It should never be loudly sniffed to provoke a sneeze.

The popularity of snuff declined during the last half of the 19th century. No one seems to know why exactly, but both Mr. Rose and Mr. Gawith speculate that the widespread introduction of white handkerchiefs around 1860 had a lot to do with it. "Snuff leaves a nicotine stain which was not noticeable on colored handkerchiefs," Mr. Rose said. "On white ones, however, it looked unattractive."

While snuff taking is not on the rise these days, it is not declining either. According to the Society of Snuff Grinders, Blenders and Purveyors, 750,000 pounds are produced in Britain each year.

"Most snuff takers use less than one ounce a week, so that's a lot of people," Mr. Rose said. "We are getting more converts all the time, especially as cigarettes get so expensive. Unlike other forms of tobacco, snuff is not taxed at all. A packet of cigarettes now costs about $1.50 while Cafe Roy ale, our most expensive because it contains pure coffee essence, is less than $3 an ounce."

Blends of snuff range from the earthy to the elegant and in many cases, such as Garden Mint, Aniseed and Carnation, their names describe their flavors. Others do not. Kendal Brown is the most "natural" snuff: it has no flavors added, only salts such as potash to hold its pungency. It is, explained Nigel Ash, a young aficionado who learned from his father, "for men, not boys, and if used injudiciously brings tears to the eyes."

Star of HBO's *True Blood* usually has some General Snus tucked above his fangs

Alexander Skarsgård, who plays broody vampire sheriff Eric Northman on HBO's hit series *True Blood*, is a closeted General snuser.

Rudy Reyes, Alexander's co-star on the *Generation Kill* series, told reporters how Skarsgård offered him some snus during a long night of partying. "It burned a hell hole in my gums so I spat it out," Reyes said.

The 6'4" Swedish actor is notoriously candid about his life offscreen, and his tobacco use is no exception. He worries that some of his younger fans may expement with snus in imitation of their screen idol. Therefore, he won't allow himself to be photographed using it.

When asked about his social status back in high school, Alexander claims that he wasn't all that popular. "I didn't stand a chance against the guys with motorcycles and a lump of snus in the ninth grade."

Yet, somewhere between the ninth grade and now, Skarsgård not only started using snus, but became really cool in the process.

Coincidence? We think not.

Catch *True Blood* every Sunday evening at 9pm, only on HBO.

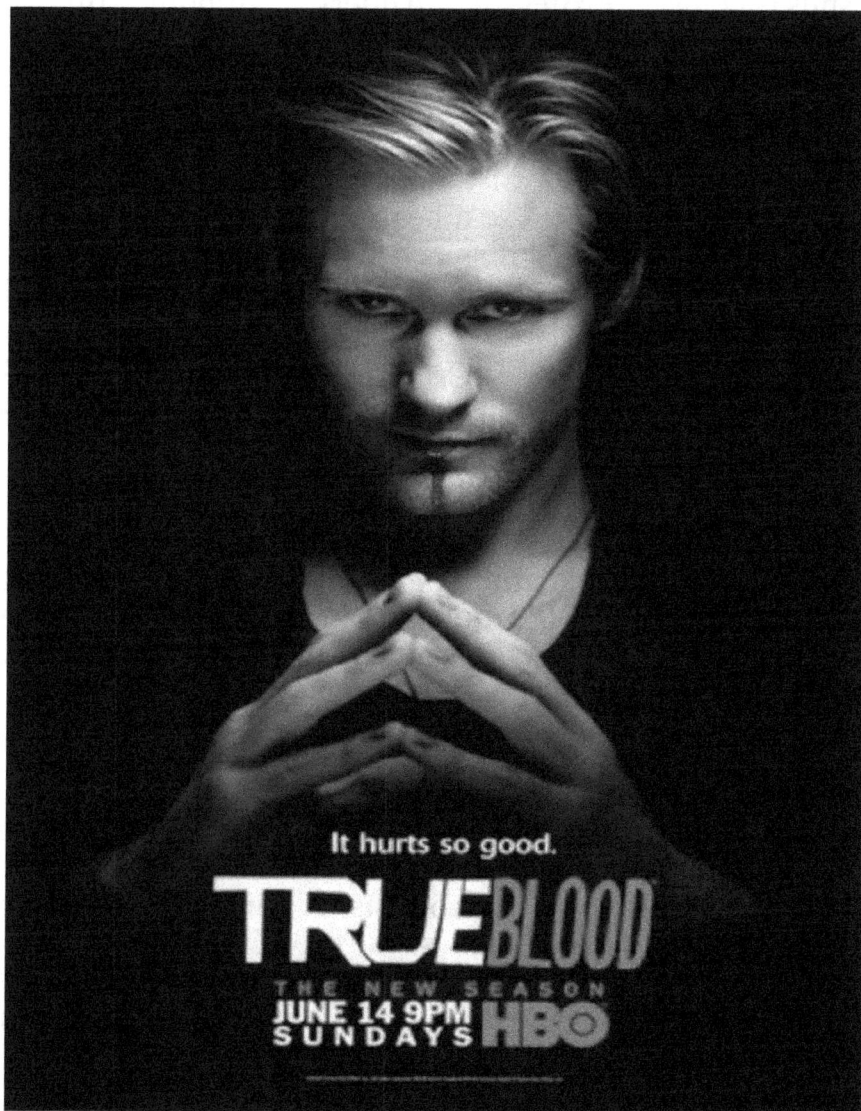

Network Europe article regarding snus; interview with Dr. Lars-Erik Rutqvist

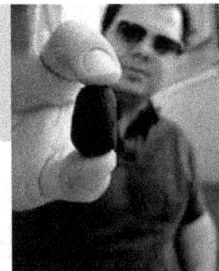

Sweden's struggle to keep its peculiar habit of oral tobacco

Sweden has been a member of the EU since 1995. But did you know that one of the most contentious issues for the Swedes during the negotiations aside from the country's much vaunted neutrality - was whether or not Swede's would be allowed to keep their peculiar habit of snus - or oral tobacco?

Now a decade has passed and snus is being marketed as a safer tobacco choice for smokers who can't quit while using conventional methods. The question is, should it be sold in other European Union member states?

The Snus War is in full swing. As Azariah Kiros explains, the conclusions of a scientific group is being used as an ammunition by both supporters and opponents of snus to claim victory.

Snus is moist, powdered tobacco which is placed under the upper lip and squeezed to extract the tobacco juice, for extended periods of time. It is manufactured, distributed, sold and consumed primarily in Sweden and Norway, although it has recently been introduced into other countries. Swedes who have developed the habit for the snus protect it jealously. But the European Union is not particularly excited by it.

When Sweden joined the Union in 1995, Swedish authorities managed to get an exemption for the use of snus in Sweden although the product was banned in the rest of the Union. The company which produces snus, Swedish Match, has been promoting the product with the argument that snus is less dangerous than smoking.

So what is the future of snus? The European Commission set up a scientific committee in an effort to answer the question. Professor Anders Ahlbom of the Karolinska Institute, a member of the Scientific group, explains the guidelines given to his Committee:

"One of them is whether or not Snus is linked to a health risk - which it is. It was asked if snus use is addictive - which it is. Then they asked us what we think would happen if snus was made available in the rest of Europe. Currently its only allowed in Sweden - it's not allowed in the other European countries."

"Then they asked if it would help to improve public health if snus was made available. And the idea is that it would help people quit smoking cigarettes and the answer it that we don't have anything that indicates that things would be better if the snus ban was struck down in the rest of Europe."

But that is not what Swedish Match, the company which produces snus and other tobacco products, is concluding from the report. It says the EU Commission's scientific committee is united in its conclusions that snus is less dangerous than smoking.

Dr. Lars Erik Rutqvist is medical spokesperson for Swedish Match:

"Up until now, the European health authorities have said that there is no scientific evidence that there are such safer tobacco products. But now in this report for the first time, a scientific committee has stated that there is such a product, that it is called *Swedish Snus,* and that it is much safer than cigarettes."

So is snus less dangerous than smoking? The Scientific Committee says it is not arguing against the claim.

"One person switching to snuff - that will probably help that person but - it is much more complex than that. You have an unknown number of former smokers who are now snus users in Sweden. And you also have a number of snus users who have never been smokers. And they would have been free from nicotine had snus not been available."

But the Swedish tobacco company says there is enough data to prove that snus is less harmful than cigarettes, and a semantic argument over statistics only hinders progress. Dr. Lars Erik Rutqvist of Swedish Match says what is important is that the EU Scientific Committee concluded that snus is a better alternative to smoking.

"It is true that snus contains nicotine, and it is therefore addictive - this is old news. And its true you cannot exclude the possibility of health risks. But an independent committee concluded unanimously that Swedish snus is much less risky than cigarettes. This is evidence that has never been backed by the scientific committee in the European Union before.

Why has the snus debate proved so controversial? The question goes first to Professor Anders Ahlbom of the EU Scientific Committee.

"Simply because the tobacco industry is very interested in selling it. They have seen that smoking is less popular and they are looking for other products to sell. The whole thing [the study]

was started by the tobacco industry to get rid of the ban in the rest of Europe. That is what is behind

this recent work. And their argument is that snus is less dangerous than cigarettes, which is true but its not really the question."

And what does the tobacco industry have to say about that? Dr. Rutqvist:

"I think the controversy is because the anti-tobacco lobby has formulated its arguments thirty years ago that all tobacco is evil - all tobacco is deadly."

"Isn't it?"

"I don't think that all tobacco is evil, no. Swedish experience has shown that the availability of a much less risky alternative can prove to be very beneficial to public health. And the Committee recognizes the fact that the availability of snus has had a positive effect on public health - no matter their personal feelings on the matter, they have to at least acknowledge the facts."

Mmm, now that's good broom-rape!

Prohibition-era book lists "known adulterations" and "filthy diseases" common in snuff brands and tobacco manufacture of the 1920's

- Cinnamon stick
- Cabbage leaves
- Grasshoppers
- Straw
- Sucking bugs
- Brown paper
- Tobacco miner
- Solution of log wood
- Broom-rape
- Licorice
- Tree cricket
- Horn worms
- Snow flea
- Moths
- Pole Burn
- Chicory leaves
- Rotten stems
- Fumigation by sulphur
- Pea Meal
- Bran
- Greenish fungus
- Sawdust
- Brown rust
- Redfield fire
- Fustic
- Fungus
- Oxide of Iron
- Black fire
- Oxide of Lead
- Field fire
- Ground Glass
- Spotted leaf
- Acorn cup
- Frenching
- Valonia
- Walloon (or Water Loon)
- Hollow stalk
- Leaves of every tree
- Tar oil
- Parasite disease
- Leaves of every plant
- Insects
- Flea Beetle
- Liquid sprays
- Orange peel
- Spices-all kinds
- Vanilla
- Valerian
- "Cigarette Beetle"
- Tonka bean
- Laudanum
- Tobacco worm
- Spanish Wine
- Cigarette Beetle
- Santa Cruz Rum
- Cutworms
- Liquors of all sorts
- Wire worm
- Morphine
- Budworm
- Antimony
- Crickets
- White Zinc
- Seaweed
- Lime
- Soda
- Dover's Powders
- Mercury
- White Lead
- Chloral Hydrate
- "Items"
- Feces
- Scrap tobacco with diseased saliva
- Copperas
- Salt of Tarter
- Sand
- Trampings from negroes' bare feet
- Alfalfa hay
- Tobacco stems
- Granulated tobacco mixed with sawdust
- Carbonate of ammonia
- Lemon peel
- Scrapings of rag pickers
- Havana flavoring
- Treacle
- Dextrin
- Green Vitriol
- Salamanca
- Resin
- Dye Woods
- Bark
- Meal
- Beet leaves
- Cabbage
- Dock
- Burdock
- Terra Japonica
- Purphiok
- Rhododendron
- Red Ochre
- Yellow Ochre
- Umber
- Red Lead
- Silica
- Bichromate of Potash
- Mould
- Salt
- Earthy Carbonates
- Iron
- Earths
- Cassia
- Columbia Root
- Gentian Root
- Colt's Foot
- Potato Skins
- Red Dyes
- Black Dyes
- Gun powder
- Opium
- Hemlock
- Nightshade
- Mice and Vermin
- Indian Hemp
- Marihuana
- Arsenic
- Bark
- Regular paper dipped in tobacco juice
- Salt peter
- Rhubarb
- Peat
- Moss
- Lampblack
- Newspaper
- Vegetable oil
- Motor oil
- Dog urine
- Poisonous pesticide
- Watermelon rind
- Deer horn
- Chicken bone
- "Fluids" from female bodily orifices
- Breadcrumbs

CALVIN D. CRANE (**BELOW**) WAS THE AUTHOR OF THE 1921 BOOK *TOBACCO: AN ASSASSIN OF LIBERTY*. AS THE HEAD OF ONE OF THE MOST VOCAL "TEMPERANCE" MOVEMENTS OF THE ERA, AND WITH ALCOHOL NOW PROHIBITED, HIS GROUP SET ITS SIGHT ON BANNING TOBACCO. HIS BOOK IS FULL OF FRUSTRATING (THOUGH HILARIOUS) LIES, MISINFORMATION, AND HYSTERICAL RAMBLINGS CONCERNING THE EVILS OF TOBACCO ADDICTION. PRINTED HERE ARE SOME OF THE MORE AMUSING ITEMS WE PICKED UP FROM MR. CRANE'S BOOK:

• Snuff users experience terrifying hallucinations.

• One man smoked a cigarette, and his hands never stopped shaking. He died shortly thereafter.

• Whores smoke cigarettes in saloons and brothels.

• Smoking leads to violent insanity in adolescents.

• Tobacco use can make you permanently blind.

• Using snuff can cause cerebral palsy in adults.

• One man overdosed on cigarettes on the street and died.

• Snuffers generally move on to cocaine or morphine after their "kicks" cease to come from nicotine.

• A train conductor spit his tobacco juice and somehow caused a derailment.

• Foreign cigars are sometimes hand-rolled by lepers. The importation of such cigars has lead to a nationwide epidemic of leprosy in cigar smokers.

• Chinese cigarettes are twelve inches long.

• Cigarettes are made by terminally ill prostitutes with venereal disease.

• Snuff contains tiny shards of glass.

• Women that take snuff do not make good companions, cooks, or wives.

• Tobacco use leads to the drinking of spirituous liquors.

• One man became so enraged after running out of tobacco that he murdered his wife.

• Chewing tobacco can harm the genitalia.

• Most chewers use enough tobacco every day to kill three non-chewers.

• Scotch snuff contains waste refuse.

• One hundred boys in London under the age of 16 died from cigarette smoking.

• One snuffer's nose rotted away.

• Foreign cigarettes are manufactured poorly, and need to be kept in hermetically sealed tins to keep from spoiling.

• One man overdosed on cigarettes in a hotel room and died.

• While locked in a room with several smokers, one man dropped dead from nicotine poisoning.

• Tobacco was a curse placed upon the white man by the 'savages' in retaliation for stealing their land.

• Tobacco's roots originated in hell, where it was created by Satan.

• Spaniards no longer participate in sporting events because tobacco has ravaged their bodies and destroyed their physical ability.

• Negro farm workers will often desecrate a tobacco plant with bodily fluids, if they believe that whites will be purchasing it.

• One man chewed tobacco that had glass in it and died.

• Leeches that bite smokers die instantly.

• Cigars and cigarettes are often drugged with poison so that the smoker can be subdued and subsequently robbed, raped, or murdered.

Ephemera was meant to be the main focus of each issue. It would combine news (both new and old) along with funny, Onion-esque articles and random reprinting of errata from the files of Tom Dunn, most of which had never seen the light of day. We later decided to keep the old stuff separate and use *Ephemera* strictly for current news and fake humor pieces. ("I can't tell which articles are real and which are fake!" exclaimed one exasperated early letter writer). The vintage stuff would be incorporated into other articles or appear under the *From The Archives* moniker.

We got a lot of feedback about the Mr. Potatohead and Dr. Calvin Crane sections in our first *Ephemera.* I think it caught a lot of readers off-guard and was probably their first indication that we weren't your typical tobacco magazine.

****

Jennifer Goldsmith was a writer friend of mine whom I had met through the now-defunct Getsnus.com forum. Getsnus.com was an American-based store that had the absolute best prices on Swedish snus. It was managed by Cigars International and partially owned by Swedish Match. When President Obama passed the PACT act, Getsnus was sold to The Northerner, who in turn deleted Getsnus's forum and instead redirected users to Snuson.com.

The Getsnus forum was small, but had a good percentage of female posters compared to Snuson or Snuscentral. Jennifer was one of these posters. Through private messaging we struck up a rapport and I wasn't at all surprised to find out that she was a writer by profession. Even though the *Ephemeris* ·was a couple of years away, I had her in mind the whole time I was plotting the first issue. Not only could we feature a female who used both snus and snuff, but she was Canadian to boot! Cool, eh?

****

David Thigpen wrote for The *Fortean Times*, which is kind of a modern-day *Ripley's Believe it or Not!* Being a distant cousin of mine, he had no problems agreeing to write an article for my new magazine (*Strange... But True!*) What he *did* have a problem with was that I expected him to write one for each subsequent issue! SBT has gone on to become one of our most popular features in the *Ephemeris,* and David still waits patiently at his mailbox for a check that will never come.

****

Anthony Haddad is pretty well-known among the snus community. His *Dr. Snus* blog is one of the most entertaining reads out there, and I called him one Sunday to see if he was interested in doing a regular column. He surprised us all by sending in *Snus Needs Supermodels!* a couple of days later. We've hung out together on numerous occasions since then and he never once fails to make me feel uncomfortably happy. Also, his wife Heather is genuinely one of the funniest people I've ever met. That's why they're both regular targets of our "fake news" pieces, where they often suffer grisly, untimely ends in situations gone awry.

CONTINUED ON PAGE 47

DIARY OF A CRAZY CAT LADY

Fevered ramblings from the mind of Jennifer Goldsmith- author, snuser, snuff taker, and crazy cat lady.

"CAT TAKING SNUFF" BY ARTHUR THEILE

I have two cats, and they're both nicotine addicts.

Now, before you start calling the ASPCA on me, let me explain. I don't condone their habit, nor do I "enable" them. Well, maybe I do... just a little.

I.

It all started about a year ago. My oldest cat, Leroy, would look up at me quizzically whenever I would grab a pinch of snuff or a pris of loose snus. He would get that sideways look about him that said "I have no idea what you're doing, but it is most intriguing. Please proceed."

After I was done handbaking my prilla or tapping a bump of snuff onto the back of my hand, Leroy would cautiously sniff my fingers. If they were coated with dry snuff, he would take a whiff and sneeze. He didn't seem to like it much,

because he would then trot off into a corner and start washing his face.

Snus was a different story, however.. Leroy cared nothing for portions, but lös caught his fancy. Whenever I cracked open a can of Göteborgs Rapé or Röda Lacket, he was all over it. No sooner than I had baked a ball, Leroy would be licking up the minuscule crumbs that had inevitably shaken loose. I tried to discourage this behavior, but Leroy wouldn't stop. I finally figured out how to keep him from eating snus; I changed brands. Leroy didn't seem to like General, and he began leaving me alone after I made the switch.

II.

About six months ago I adopted a girl kitty that I named Ivy. Whereas Leroy seemed ambivalent towards nasal snuff, Ivy loved it. She would lick it up off the table or off of my fingertips. She would sniff an open can until she sneezed, then she would back off for a minute or two and do it again. Sniffing up the crumbs didn't bother me, but when she started licking up the minuscule crumbs that had inevitably shaken loose. I tried to discourage this behavior, but Leroy wouldn't stop. I finally figured out how to keep him from eating snus; I changed brands. Leroy didn't seem to like General, and he began leaving me alone after I made the switch.

II.

About six months ago I adopted a girl kitty that I named Ivy. Whereas Leroy seemed ambivalent towards nasal snuff, Ivy loved it. She would lick it up off the table or off of my fingertips. She would sniff an open can until she sneezed, then she would back off for a minute or two and do it again. Sniffing up the crumbs didn't bother me, but when she started licking it out of the tin like it was some sort of kitty treat, well... I was a little concerned.

I contacted my vet with my dilemma. I guess they thought I was trying to be funny, because I was told that "Cats don't like tobacco. Period." Uh... ok. So I contacted an online vet that is supposed to be some sort of cat whisperer, or

some such nonsense. She told me that "Tobacco is just as carcinogenic to cats as it is to humans. The nicotine will kill your cats! It is a poison." Gee, thanks lady. I just wanted to know if this was normal behavior in some cats, not to get a lecture about how horrible I am for letting my cats use snuff.

So then I contacted the Professor of Veterinary Sciences at my local community college. I didn't hear back from him at first, so I thought that he, too, must think me a crank. However, about a week later I got a very nice emailed response from him:

Dear Jennifer,

Don't feel bad for your cats developing what seems to be a tobacco habit. Cats love stimulants

just as much as humans do- hence the brisk sale of cat nip. The nicotine in tobacco is much the same as the effect that they would receive from the catmint plant, so I wouldn't worry too much about it.

I would try to limit their intake though, because nicotine in large doses is of course fatal. From what you've shared, they don't take enough to cause any concern. If you notice a change in their diet or bowel movements, I would cease allowing them to eat any more snuff.

Cats develop strange tastes. I would not say that this is normal for most cats, but I did have a patient's cat several years ago that developed a taste for pipe tobacco. The cat lived to the ripe old age of 18, so who knows. It may have been the pipe tobacco that was keeping him healthy!

Sincerely,

Dr. Richardson

So there you go, PETA. I'm not such a horrible person after all.

III.

A couple of weeks after the letter arrived, I was cleaning the house when I came across something strange. Tucked behind the recliner was a tin of Berwick Brown that had gone missing last year. The lid was missing, and so was most of the snuff. While trying to figure out how the tin got to its unusual hiding place, another question came to me- how did it end up perfectly upright with the lid removed? And were those whisker marks on the outer edge of the tin?

I had a vision of devious cats waiting for me to go to sleep,

then pocketing my snuff can and hiding it behind the chair. For the life of me, I can only guess to how they would have opened it (since, according to Robert De Niro, cats lack opposable thumbs)

knobs.

At least now I have an explanation for my cats running wild all hours of the night. They waited for me to go to bed, and then got all hopped up on snuff. That would also explain why they always seemed to have brown, crusty snot early in the morning.

I guess I've set a bad example for them.

JENNIFER GOLDSMITH IS A FREELANCE WRITER BASED OUT OF TORONTO. WHILE NOT BUSY SMUGGLING SNUS AND SNUFF ACROSS THE BORDER, SHE TAKES CARE OF TWO VERY FAT CATS. SHE CAN BE REACHED VIA SNAIL MAIL AT THE FOLLOWING ADDRESS:

JENNIFER GOLDSMITH - C/O THE EPHEMERIS - PO BOX 287- SPRING LAKE, NC 28390 - USA

STE

STRANGE...

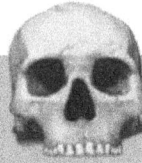

BY DAVID THIGPEN

BUT TRUE!

Monkeying Around

A monkey was arrested for smoking a cigarette in South Bend, Indiana in 1924. The monkey went to trial, was found guilty, and fined 25.00 plus court costs.

The monkey was a performance artist that belonged to a local organ grinder. The organ grinder explained to the court that by teaching the monkey to smoke, he was attempting to generate more publicity for their act.

It's unclear if the simian citizen paid his fine but to this day it is still illegal to make a monkey smoke a cigarette in South Bend.

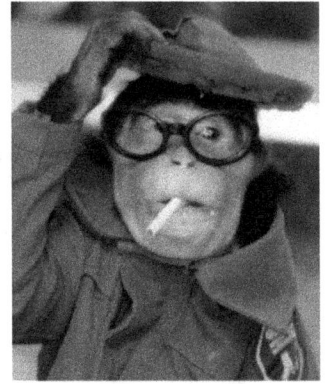

Local South Bend, IN resident Cornelius Van Zant baffled by discriminatory smoking law still on the books. "Bars, restaurants, and public buildings, I can sort of understand. But now they're telling me I can't smoke PERIOD? See, this is the reason I vote libertarian."

Each issue we bring you the strangest, wackiest, most bizarre tobacco - related anecdotes that our researchers could find. From odd laws to bumbling mishaps, we guarantee that it's all TRUE!

Not up to snuff...

The Abani Tribe of Nigeria love their snuff. However, the recipes that they use would make the average Westerner green... and not with envy!

The tribal medicine man concocts a tincture from Jaguar urine and dried dung beetles. Warmed over a fire, the resulting mess is ground into a fine powder with a carved rasp, shaped like a phallus. The tribesmen then snuff the compound, which they believe gives them strong sexual prowess.

THE SAD TALE OF TOPSY, THE HOMICIDAL ELEPHANT

Topsy the Elephant (1875-1903) was a trained circus elephant that tired of performing for audiences. In 1900, she killed her trainer by stomping him to death and did the same to his replacement a year later.

Her next trainer, J.F. Blount, was quite cruel to the elephant and attempted to make her appear stupid before a crowd of onlookers by feeding her a lit cigarette. Topsy rejected the cigarette and trampled Blount to death, to the horror of the viewers in attendance.

Her owners decided that Topsy was too dangerous to be kept alive, and they scheduled her to die by hanging in late 1902. The ASPCA intervened and demanded a more humane method of execution. Thomas Edison volunteered to electrocute the elephant using alternating current, as had been the preferred method of executing condemned criminals for the last twelve years.

On January 4th, 1903, Topsy was electrocuted in front of a large crowd at Coney Island's Luna Park. Her final meal consisted of sweet carrots laced with potassium cyanide . The event was recorded by Edison and released to theaters under the title "Electrocuting an Elephant".

This event marked the grand opening of Luna Park, which suffered an unusual amount of strange accidents in the ensuing years. Bizarre catastrophes were often blamed on the restless spirit of Topsy. Luna Park closed down in 1943, after a series of mysterious fires that were dubbed "Topsy's Revenge".

On July 20, 2003, a hundred years after her death, a memorial for Topsy was erected at the Coney Island Museum. Luna Park was reopened on May 29th, 2010. We hope, for the park's sake, that Topsy is finally at peace!

So, to clarify:

Giving a monkey a cigarette will land you a fine. Giving an elephant a cigarette will get you killed.

Check.

ELEPHANT ELECTROCUTED FOR MURDER.

The photograph shows Topsy, the elephant electrocuted at Coney Island for murdering three men. A current of 6400 volts was used. Topsy was the original baby elephant.

Marlboros are for sissies!

Marlboro cigarettes, the best selling smoke in the world, used to be a "chick'" cigarette.

"Marlborough" Cigarettes were first sold by Philip Morris in 1902, and its sales remained unremarkable up until 1924, when "Marlboro" cigarettes, in a stroke of marketing genius, was relaunched as a woman's brand- one of the first in the nation.

Dubbed "Mild as May" and featuring a crimson-colored cork tip to help hide lipstick smudges, the brand languished in obscurity for another thirty years before being repackaged as a "macho" smoke.

So, the next time one of your buddies lights up a Cowboy Killer, ask him if the filter helps to obscure his lipstick smears! (Hint: Don't do this unless your buddy is much smaller and less powerful than you.)

Göteborg physicians K. Knudsen and M. Strinnholm reported the case of a 42-year-old man who self-administered 75 portions of snus into his anus.

After inserting the three cans worth of snus into his rectum, the man began passing out intermittently and vomiting uncontrollably. He drove himself to the hospital, where the physicians diagnosed his situation as "life-threatening." His blood pressure had reached a dangerous high and he was dehydrated.

After the snus was removed, he was hooked up to an artificial breathing apparatus for twelve hours, and held for another day while his condition was monitored. He was released later the following morning..

No explanation was ever given as to why the man inserted 75 snus portions into his sphincter.

The physicians concluded that "excessive rectal administration of moist snuff may be life threatening."

Lightning in a Barn

The most people ever killed by a single bolt of lightning were eight North Carolina tobacco farm workers in the summer of 1961.

The men were picking tobacco when the lightning storm began, and they took refuge in the closest curing barn. The lightning struck a piece of the tin roof, traveled down a pipe that was attached to the wall, then finally connected with a metal grate that the men were standing on. They died instantly. It is estimated that the odds of such a feat ever occurring again naturally are 1 in 18 billion.

These smokes pack a punch!

As reported by the BBC, an Indonesian man was smoking a cigarette when it exploded in his face, knocking out six of his teeth. The smoker, 31-year-old Andi Susanto settled out of court with PT Nojorono Tobacco, the company that manufactured the cigarette. They awarded him the sum of $535.00 USD and paid his medical bills.

It is still not known what actually caused the cigarette to explode, and scientific analysis of its remnants have proven to be inconclusive. None of this matters to Susanto, who is just happy to have his teeth back. He claims that he was trying to quit smoking anyway.

DAVID THIGPEN IS A FORMER WRITER FOR THE FORTEAN TIMES. HE IS NOT A CAT.

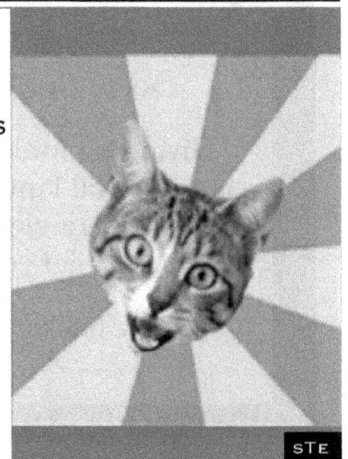

STE

Snus Needs Supermodels !

Commentary by Anthony Haddad

On a recent trip to a local mega-liquor store, I stopped by their tobacco section as I'd heard there was a General snus refrigerator there. Sitting on a high shelf outside of the humidor was their snus fridge. It was one of the big black metal refrigerators with doors on the front and back – a sharp looking display unit, in my opinion.

Inside was one can of General Loose with an expiration date from 2009. Almost a year out of date.

Why had they not reordered snus? Was this happening in other stores? Could we attribute this to corporate bureaucracy in the shops? Or was it a response to lack of demand?

Looking for answers, I rang up a buddy of mine who manages one of these liquor mega-stores. I asked him what the deal was. He told me that snus didn't sell well for them, and that the expiration date made it a difficult choice to invest in a product that wasn't moving.

Shortly after I had spoken with him, a Swedish Match sales rep stopped by the cigar shop my wife and I own and where we carry General snus. He said,"You're selling these really well. None of them are expired."

That's a pretty low bar for selling well.

But, let's back up. What General has been saying for years is that they got into cigar shops because tobacconists would be able to explain what snus was to their customers. This is opposed to convenience stores, where the sales clerk doesn't really need to know a thing about tobacco other than know where the Marlboros Lights are stored, and perhaps which end of it to light.

But there is a small problem. Most tobacco shops are really cigar shops that may or may not have some hard-to-find smokes and man knickknacks. And cigar shops have minimal interest in pushing any tobacco product other than cigars to their existing customers.

The logic here is pretty simple. A standard high quality, handmade cigar costs about $8.00, the wholesale price is about half that. Snus runs about $4.50, and the wholesale price is again about half. (State taxes can change these numbers dramatically, so these numbers just consider federal taxes.) So you make a little more money on the sale of one cigar than one tin of snus. More important than the price, however, is that a cigar lasts just one or two hours while a tin of snus can last a couple days to a week. That's a threat to a cigar shop's revenue.

So when an existing, cigar-smoking customer comes in, points to the General fridge and asks, "What's that?" The tobacconist would be an idiot to say anything other than, "That's some weird foreign dip. Let me show you to our cigars."

What's more, General Cigar Co. and their sales team probably felt the same way about snus. They were already making money. Why push something that could potentially cannibalize sales? You don't. You object to the idea, and when the suits tell you to do it anyway, you do it poorly. Then when sales suck, you go back to them and say, "I told you so."

General's goal by the end of 2010 is to have snus in 1,200 stores , that means Swedish Match has given away at least 1,200 refrigerators and 60,000 tins of snus, plus samples and promotional material. One could argue they haven't gotten snus in enough stores yet, but if they were in 120,000 stores, they would have had to give away 120,000 refrigerators and 600,000 tins of snus with no guarantee of any better results.

Perhaps the real question is not "Is Swedish Match doing enough to promote snus in the US?", but rather, given the lack of motivation by tobacconists to push snus on their customers, "Did Swedish Match choose the right distribution channel?"

It looks like Swedish Match is asking

themselves the same thing. In the spring of 2010, I got a text message from a friend of mine. "Just saw General snus at Speedy Stop Gas Station." This went against what General had been saying all along. By midsummer, General was in five of these c-stores in the Austin, Texas, area.

Then news came that General snus was no longer in the hands of General Cigar; Swedish Match North America was taking over. Since Swedish Match North America is in pretty much every convenience store in the U.S., one might guess that a broader distribution may be in the works. However, a Swedish Match sales rep told me that the Speedy Stop gas stations are a test market and they aren't moving very well in convenience stores.

It seems to me that America just doesn't understand snus. Unless supermodels, baseball players, and the cast of *Jersey Shore* start snusing, mainstream America will be slow to get onboard. That's why I've taken it upon myself to send a letter to Gary Coleman asking him to be the official spokesperson for snus.

I'll let you know when I hear back...

STE

Bygone Brands

The Flavors of Yesteryear

Featured this month: **Rocker Snus**

Poor, misunderstood Rocker.

Rocker AB started producing snus in early 2000. Their warehouse was an old dairy farm that had been converted for use as a snus factory.

Rocker sought to reach the same demographic that Skruf had successfully stolen away from Swedish Match- young, urbanized snusers that wanted a "hip" brand that they could identify with.

Rocker attempted to distance itself from the other brands on the market with its retro chic ovular-shaped tin that had fallen out of favor during the early sixties. The cans lacked any printed labeling; the color of the tin was the only indicator of the contents inside.

The brand launched with two "colors"- Red and **Black**. **Black** was a traditional General-type citrus and bergamot flavored snus (think: Olde Viking Black), while the Red attempted more of an Ettan/Grov "neutral" vibe. (When the Rocker factory was later purchased by PMI, **Black** received a facelift and became *Philip Morris 1847*.)

One aspect of the Rocker line was its strong chemical scent, one that has been described as being reminiscent of cat urine or ammonia. Various theories abound as to what produces this smell in certain tobacco products, but Rocker's official explanation was that its product was so fresh that it gave off a pungent scent directly after breaking its "hermetic" seal. (Indeed, Rocker was advertised as not needing refrigeration due to this "revolutionary" new packaging technique.)

Later additions to the Rocker lineup were introduced over the following six years:

• **Silver** was a "frosted" type snus (think: Offroad Frosted)

• **Blue** had an aniseed and licorice flavor (think: Jak's/ Gotlandssnus Grey)

• **Gold** was an attempt at creating the world's first coffee-flavored snus. Very similar to Offroad's later Coffee-Vanilla.

• **Green** was a mini-portion with a Rapé-styled juniper and berry mix (think: LD Blue, Thunder Blue).

• And finally, there was Rocker **White**, which was the company's only foray into the then-new world of white portions. It was, essentially, a dumbed-down Rocker **Black** in a dryer pouch.

The new flavors (for the most part) failed to catch on, and Rocker was soon scaled down to just two brands, **Black** and Silver. By 2006, Rocker Production AB had hit dire straits and shut its doors for good. When they folded, they accounted for a mere 0.1% of the total snus market worldwide.

The factory and its holdings were then purchased by Philip Morris International. With an eye towards entering the worldwide snus market, PMI revamped Rocker **Black** and Rocker White with a snazzy new metal can design and rechristened it '1847 by Philip Morris.'

PMI later merged with Swedish Match, which made the manufacture of **1847** at the old Rocker factory somewhat redundant. Swedish Match closed the doors and started their own production of the **1847** snus.

SM tweaked the recipe and gave **1847** a new tin design, but it failed to catch on in the Swedish snus market. To the dismay of a handful of American buyers, **1847** ceased production on June 1st, 2010.

It seems that we've heard the last of Rocker Snus for now, but only time will tell if some vestige of the old name shows up down the road in some form or fashion...

STE

Remembering Fribourg & Treyer

A. PHILLIPS GRIFFITHS IS PROFESSOR OF PHILOSOPHY AT THE UNIVERSITY OF WARWICK, COVENTRY, ENGLAND. HIS WEBSITE, WWW.SNUFFBOX.ORG.UK, WAS ONE OF THE FIRST NASAL SNUFF SITES ON THE WEB, DEBUTING IN 1998.

They had a beautiful shop with bow windows at the upper end of the Haymarket, as well as other shops in the Burlington Arcade, Oxford, and Cambridge.

They were pipe & tobacco specialists as well as Britain's premier snuff chandler.

My first encounter was when I went up to Oxford as a graduate in 1951. Entering their lovely shop at 130 High Street, I asked the little man in charge "Do you sell snuff by the quarter ounce?".

Drawing himself up to his full height (nearly 5 feet) he glared up at me. "Sir, this is a snuff shop! We sell snuff, not dust beaten up from the carpet. This University is going to the dogs!" I hesitantly explained that I wanted to test & try a variety of snuffs, rather than risk all of my few coppers on only one. "Test and try as many as you like!" he said, opening up the boxes on display one after another .

I will not say we became friends, but I think he thought of himself as my mentor on many subsequent visits when he would authoritatively expand on the character & virtues of the various snuffs.

He must be dead now; as is (the original) Fribourg and Treyer.

Ironically, John Arlott (1974) ends his book by saying of Fribourg & Treyer, "*One of its traditions is sheer business acumen... A survival such as that of Fribourg and Treyer in the jungle of mercantile London can never be fortuitous.*"

It was bought by Imperial Tobacco, which apparently could not afford to renew the lease on the Haymarket premises, and after briefly moving it to Regent Street closed it down. At least, Imperial Tobacco sold the Fribourg & Treyer line-up of snuff-making recipes to Wilsons of Sharrow, who still make its excellent Bordeaux snuff.

F&T snuff is the oldest continuously manufactured tobacco product in the world. Here's to another 300 years! STE

FRIBOURG and TREYER
(Est. 1720 in Haymarket, London)
Tobacconists and Purveyors of Foreign Snuffs
TO THEIR LATE MAJESTIES
The Kings of Hanover and Belgium
Their Late Royal Highnesses
THE DUKES OF SUSSEX, CAMBRIDGE and DUCHESS OF KENT

DIRTY HERO:

REMEMBERING Curt Jürgens

Sadly, like most of the world's greatest actors, Curt Jürgens is hardly a household name.

Appearing in over 150 different films, Jürgens is perhaps best remembered today by English-speaking audiences as the prototypical Bond villain Karl Stromberg in 1977's *The Spy Who Loved Me;* a role in which he was loath to take if not for the paycheck involved. Jürgens, like several of his contempraries (Lawrence Olivier, John Carradine and Henry Fonda among them) wished to be remembered primarily as a stage actor, though the overwhelming bulk of their work was actually in film.

In this article, we take a look at not only Curt Jürgens the actor, but Curt Jürgens the *snuffer.* Aside from acting, snuff was perhaps his greatest passion, and one that he is not generally remembered for.

Standing 6'4" and speaking with a distinctive Teutonic accent, Jürgens had an undeniable stage presence.

He made films in over a dozen countries and could act in six different languages. Highly educated and extremely well read, his IQ was reported to be at near-genius level. His wit was legendary, and he had no time for those he considered intellectual "weaklings."

One of his wives once remarked that "there are only two things that Curd never left the house without–a linen handkerchief and a tin of Bernard snuff. Of this, he was fanatical."

This is his story.

41

EARLY LIFE

He was born Curd Gustav Gottlieb Franz Jürgens in Munich on December 13th, 1915 to a German caviar salesman and a French schoolmarm. His father was a stern disciplinarian, while his mother was a more free-spirited liberal. The two contrasting extremes imbued with Jürgens a strange juxtaposition that did not go unnoticed by his close friends. Said Charles Kay: "One evening he was railing against the Church, positively venomous slurs against organized religion. The next day he said something to the effect that the Catholic Church was the best thing to happen to Africa, since they could teach the heathens how to be civilised."

As a teenager, Curt was aware of the growing Nazi sentiment that was threatening to take over his homeland. "I thought it was all silly," he wrote. "Nationalism, Norse pride, survival of the fittest... these were all ideals that were resurrected in order to gain control of the populace. I was ashamed at how stupid my fellow Germans were. Those that bought into it."

Jürgens, who was studying journalism, began writing for a liberal newspaper that operated out of Munich. It was during this time that he met his first wife, the actress Louise Basler. She encouraged Curt to pursue a career in acting; a dream that he had entertained since childhood.

"I was writing for a newspaper, which was considered (just barely) a 'real' job... but my wife earned more money on stage in one week than I made all month. Yet acting was not a man's profession. I was torn between being a man and being an actor. In the end, the money won out over all." Wishing to leave his native Bavaria, the couple relocated to Vienna, Austria. There, Jürgens built a name for himself acting on stage.

In 1935, Jürgens appeared in his first film, *The Waltz King*, and from then on he turned out a steady body of work over the course of the next decade. To his dismay, he was becoming more famous for his movie roles than he was his stage performances. He was loath to make films, but again, "the money was just too good to pass up." He continued to perform theatrically as often as his schedule would allow.

WORLD WAR II. NAZIS. THE FIFTIES.

Fed up with the rise of Nazism in his own country, Jürgens relocated to Hungary in order to continue his career in the midst of the War. When Germany seized control in 1944, Jürgens was sent to a concentration camp for "political unreliables." There he remained until the close of the war, not appearing in another film until 1948. Upon his release, he formally renounced his German citizenship and became a legal resident of Austria. He and his wife divorced shortly after. He was remarried to Austrian actress Judith Holzmeister in 1947.

Jürgens returned to films with an eagerness that had been lacking prior to his imprisonment. Committed to making his new marriage work, he desired the regular income that only film work seemed to bring.

Like many post-war German actors, he found steady work in English-language cinema. There was a great demand for German actors, who often portrayed Nazi soldiers in Hollywood war films. Curt was no exception. Usually billed as the anglicized *Curt Jurgens*, he appeared in films and TV productions, usually playing the typical spy or Nazi officer.

Though hardly a household name in the US, starring roles in such features las *Bitter Victory* and *The Enemy Below* helped to solidify his credentials among American filmmakers.

In 1955, Jürgens left his second wife and married Hungarian actress Eva Bartok. The two-year marriage was, by all accounts, stormy. The couple produced one daughter together, Deana Jurgens. Shortly after her birth, Jürgens left his wife and newborn child in a move that the press dubbed "callous, rude, and evil." However, the truth about the Bartok-Jürgens marriage wasn't revealed until nearly thirty years later.

In 1933, Jürgens was injured in a terrible car wreck. The accident severed his spermatic cords, which left him unable to produce children. Thus, when Bartok (whom Jürgens had long suspected of having an affair) suddenly became pregnant in 1956, her infidelity was no longer questionable. It was revealed in 1987 that Deana Jurgens was actually fathered by Frank Sinatra, a charge that Sinatra himself would neither confirm nor deny.

1956 brought him his biggest role to date, in Roger Vadim's *...and God Created Woman*. Starring alongside Brigitte Bardot, the film went on to become an international success.

Curt was remarried in 1958 to Simone Bicheron, whom he called "the love of my life- the only wife I ever really had." They stayed married for almost twenty years. During that time they lived all over the world, with the Jürgens' owning homes in Vienna, Paris, the Bahamas, Zurich and New York.

THE SIXTIES AND SEVENTIES. A DESCENT INTO HELL.

In 1962, Jurgens landed the part of Major General Blumentritt in the war epic *The Longest Day.* The role helped to cement his stature as an international film star. Though somewhat overshadowed by the dozens of other stars featured in the Darryl F. Zanuck spectacle, Jürgens' part was quite memorable, and it helped him garner more parts in subsequent Hollywood productions.

The sixties were a mixed bag of career highlights and questionable film choices. Notable appearances in *Lord Jim* and *Battle of Britain* were offset by low-budget fare like *Bedroom Stewardesses, Dirty Heroes,* and *An Affair of States*.

In 1970, Jürgens suffered a major heart attack while filming a movie in France. A self-avowed agnostic earlier in life, the experience made him question his entire belief system. He claimed to have suffered a Near Death Experience in which his soul traveled to hell. Surrounded by eyeless, mouthless demons that clawed at him and attempted to drag him deeper into the dark abyss, Curt was revived on the operating table an instant before the creatures could carry him off.

The experience left him a firm believer in the afterlife, and he committed himself to living a more pious existence. Wanting to discard his most destructive habits, Curt eliminated cigarettes and alcohol from his daily regimen. (Though he sometimes appeared onstage with a cigarette after his heart attack, he had stopped smoking them completely in his personal life. He still favored the occasional pipe or cigar from time to time, though.)

CURT TEACHES HIS NEW WIFE (ALGERIAN FASHION MODEL SIMONE BICHERON) HOW TO LIGHT HIS PIPE.

He preferred snuff to smoking anyway, often trying to convince friends to give up cigarettes in favor of nasal snuff. Whenever a fellow actor would light up, Jürgens was close by with a tin of snuff and an invitation to sample it.

"This is how real men, men of dignity, take their tobacco," he is quoted as saying to one film journalist.

Jürgens preferred German dry snuff, but he was known to take British, Swedish and Polish snuff as well. He frowned upon American snuff, which he considered inferior, and looked down upon the Swedish, who took their snus orally. "The Swede chews his snuff like a cow chews its cud, and looks equally insipid in the process."

Perhaps inspired by his recent brush with death, Curt managed to squeeze in a few supernatural thrillers throughout the seventies. It was a genre that he previously refused to act in, saying that "[Horror films] are cheap thrills for teenagers and those of sub-par intellect." Regardless, his performances in *The Vault of Horror*, *The Mephisto Waltz,* and *Cagliostro* rank among some of his best work.

In 1976, Jürgens penned his autobiography, *. . . und kein bisschen weise (...And Not a Bit Wise)*. Full of candid anecdotes involving well-known actors and actresses, it was an early example of the "celebrity tell-all" that became so popular in the following decade. The book was attacked by the international film industry as well as the press, who found it to be "excessively gossip-ish... less an autobiography and more a scandal rag." Unshaken, Jürgens responded that if anyone was upset about the way they were portrayed in his book, "they shouldn't have acted that way in the first place."

The following year, Jürgens made perhaps his best known contribution to film in *The Spy Who Loved Me*, the third James Bond outing for Roger Moore and the biggest budgeted of the series to date. Though his memorable portrayal of supervillian Karl Stromberg was well received by both the public and the press, Jürgens was highly critical of his role, and of the Bond series in general. He felt that they were "children's movies", and considered it a blemish on his career to have to appear in such "comic book fantasies".

The Spy Who Loved Me went on to be the largest grossing Bond film since the Connery era, and was one of the highest earning films of the decade .The film lead to a renewed interest in Curt Jürgens career, and he was soon asked to play Siegmund Freud in the 1979 telefilm *Bergasse 19*. The part of Freud was one that he had played before onstage, and it was said to have been his most favorite role.

The Eighties. The End.

CURT ENJOYS A PINCH OF SCHMALZER BACKSTAGE WITH CO-STAR NICOLE HEESTERS. AUSTRIA, 1973

The eighties opened on a positive note for Jürgens, who appeared in such diverse films as the offbeat alien invasion pic *Why UFO's Steal Our Lettuce*, the gothic/horror character study *The Sleep of Death*, and the title role in 1981's *Collin*. In 1982, he had a supporting role in the BBC adaptation of John Le Carré's *Smiley's People*, starring alongside Alec Guinness. It was to be his final role.

On June 18th, 1982, Curt Jürgens suffered a massive heart attack at his home in Vienna. He left behind his fifth wife, Margie Schmitz, whom he had married in 1978. The 66- year-old's death came as a shock in Europe, where his obituary was plastered across newspapers and magazines throughout the continent. Many actors spoke on his behalf, including Brigitte Bardot, who called Jürgens the "handsomest man I've ever worked with."

He left behind an incredible body of work, one that is only now beginning to achieve cult status, almost thirty years after his death. Whether you consider him a great actor, an intriguing writer, or the second-most sexiest actor of our time (according to a 2005 German tabloid poll), there's no denying that Curt was one-of-a-kind.

We here at the *Ephemeris* choose to recall Curt Jürgens as a pioneer. An early, vocal proponent of reduced -harm tobacco use, Jürgens made snuff taking look fashionable at a time when it wasn't.

Whenever you watch a Curt Jürgens film, look hard at the outfit he is wearing on screen. More often than not, you can see the outline of a snuffbox pressing through his pocket.   sTE

GERMAN STAMP COMMEMORATING CURT JURGENS.

Selected Filmography

Curt Jurgens made many movies in his day, and not all of them were classics. He often referred to himself as "The German John Carradine." Yet even in the most horrible of these films, he never failed to give a Grade-A performance. Listed below are some of his better roles or "important" movies that made film scholars sit up and take notice when the public ignored them.

1935-1947

Konigswalzer (1935)

The Unknown (1936)

Salonwagen E 417 (1939)

Operette (1940)

Wen die Gotter lieben (Who the Gods Love) (1942)

A Fortunate Man (1943)

A Look Back (1944)

A Little Summer Melody (1944)

As the cunning strategist Major General Gunther Blumentritt in Twentieth Century Fox's *The Longest Day* (1962).

1958-1969

Inn of the 6th Happiness ('58)

The Blue Angel (1959)

Brainwashed (1960)

Disorder (1962)

The Longest Day (1962)

Hide and Seek (1964)

Target for Killing (1966)

Dirty Heroes (1967)

Battle of Britain (1969)

1948-1957

The Singing House (1948)

Lambert Is Threatened (1949)

The Disturbed Wedding Night (1950)

My Life is at Stake (1951)

April 1st, **2000** (1952)

Music By Night (1953)

The Last Waltz (1953)

Orient Express (1954)

The Devil's General (1955)

Love Without Illusions (1955)

House of Intrigue (1956)

Devil in Silk (1956)

The Golden Bridge (1956)

... And God Created Woman (1956)

Michael Strogoff (1956)

Bitter Victory (1957)

An Eye for an Eye (1957)

The Enemy Below (1957)

1970-1982

The Invincible Six (1970)

Kill! Kill! Kill! Kill! (1971)

The Mephisto Waltz (1971)

Nicholas and Alexandria (1971)

War is Hell (1972)

The Vault of Horror (1973)

Radiograph of a Swastika (1974)

Fall of Eagles (TV, 1974)

The Spy Who Loved Me (1977)

Missile X (1978)

Just a Gigolo (1978)

Berggasse 19 (TV, 1979)

Breakthrough (1979)

Goldengirl (1979)

Assassination Attempt (1981)

The Sleep of Death (1981)

Collin (TV, 1981)

Smiley's People (TV, 1982)

Bygone Brands was intended to be a regular feature, but it usually always ends up on the chopping block by the time we go to print. Hopefully we'll run more of this series in future volumes. Rocker was one of the first snus brands I ever tried and it was pretty fun researching its brief production.

****

When I first began using nasal snuff, pretty much the only online resource regarding the subject was Professor A. Phillips Griffiths' *snuffbox.org.uk* website, which debuted in 1998. Professor Griffiths is probably the world's foremost authority on nasal snuff. Sadly, his work schedule keeps him too busy to pen new material for the STE, but he graciously allowed us to reprint any of his articles that we wished, and we chose the Fribourg & Treyer piece for this issue.

****

The Curt Jurgens bio was probably the oldest article in the book. I wrote it about two years earlier for Snuscentral, but I never really thought it would fit well there. After all, there was only one quote about snus in the entire piece, and it was pretty derogatory. I had a few articles like these piled up that I tried shopping around to mainstream magazines, who didn't have a use for them either. I decided to sit on them until I found a suitable outlet.

Celebrity snuff users intrigue me to no end. I was impressed after reading Jurgens' autobiography to learn that he was such an avid tobagophile that I felt I needed to share it with the rest of the world. This article, more than any other, opened the floodgates in terms of our shamelessness in approaching the associates of celebrities for information regarding their tobacco habits. It also helps that we have a couple of staff writers who are "connected" to the industry and can land us a quote or a phone call from the big shots. By our sixth issue, we had people contacting *us* with info. "I'm so and so and I'm the great grand-niece of [Hollywood B-actor from the 50's] and did you know that he was a big snuff user?" It's probably my favorite thing about being part of this magazine.

****

A very nice lady sent me a letter once through the Snuscentral site trying to find out more information about a particular "haunted"snuff mill she grew up near. After a brief correspondence, she shared the story in this issue and I was so intrigued I built an article around it. We still get letters from people to this day asking us if we believe in ghosts (probably) or if we're just plain stupid (yes.)

****

Quackery! is an ongoing feature that is a blatant rip-off of Penn & Teller's *Bullsh!t*. Digging through the archives, it's amazing to find ads for stuff like "Doctor Richmond's Asthma Cigarettes" and "Baltimore's Own Nicotine Cure" (active ingredients: cocaine and morphine). But every now and then we come across a website selling sugar pills that promise to cure lung cancer or something, and we feel the need to take these bastards to task for their, uh... quackery.

CONTINUED ON PAGE 70

Ye Olde Haunted Snuff Mill?

Strange occurrences rumored to transpire at abandoned New Jersey snuff factory

The Ephemeris received a letter from a Mrs. G. Hoffman of Fishkill, NY, shortly before going to press. We present the letter here in its entirety; its interpretation rests solely in the minds of our readers.

If anyone out there has any information regarding the Cedar Grove Snuff Mill, please drop us a line at the address listed at the end of the article.

Dear Mr. Hubbard,

Perhaps you can help me with something that's been bugging me for the last sixty odd years!

When I was a little girl my family lived in Cedar Grove, NJ and on the east side of town there was this really old snuff mill there. This was back in the depression times, thirties and forties, and we children didn't have much to do in those days except play around.

Well, this old mill was abandoned for God knows how long, and all of the kids would dare each other to go in the mill or to spend the night in there. It was supposed to be haunted by the ghost of the man that built it, and there was a story going around that he had killed his family and burned down the plant with himself inside of it.

Supposedly, at night you could see his ghost inside of the mill looking out of the window, and rumor had it that there were several kids that went in the mill and were never seen again.

FUN FACT: Cedar Grove's major claim to fame is that the crossword puzzle was invented there in 1913.

were never seen or heard from again. I do recall that two of the boys I went to school with in the third grade disappeared just weeks apart from each other, and they were never found. It was rumored that they were victims of serial killer Albert Fish, who was apprehended a couple of years later.

One night me and my girlfriend Anna were coming home late from a music recital at the school. It was a Friday night around Halloween. I don't know if the time of the season had anything to do with it, but we had to pass by the mill to get to Anna's house, and on this particular night it was pitch black outside. There weren't any street lights then and that block was pretty much abandoned, so it was extra spooky going by there after dark.

Well, we were passing by feeling scared, and Anna bent down to tie her shoe. We were right in front of the mill, and I kept telling her to hurry up! Then all of the sudden Anna pointed up and said "look!" and I turned to the mill. A big burst of light came from inside the building, and shone through all of the windows in the mill. It was like a fireworks show was going on inside.

And then, on the bottom row of windows (on the first floor), we could see the shadow of a very tall man walking back and forth really fast, like he was in the middle of some important task. We both screamed! We were so scared!

Then, as quickly as it started, it all stopped. It was like someone had flicked a light switch on for about five seconds, and then turned it off. That's how long it lasted, about five seconds.

Me and Anna took off as fast as we could and got to her house, ran in and locked the door. Her older sister was home, and we told her what happened. She laughed at us at first, but when we broke down in tears, she knew we weren't fibbing. We told our parents about it and my ma just told me not to go past the mill after dark.

This was when I was about twelve or thirteen, and I never forgot it. Me and Anna stayed friends all through high school and up into college, and we would sometimes tell our boyfriends about what we saw that night. Sometimes they would think we were kidding, but some of the time they would turn kind of white thinking about the old haunted mill in Cedar Grove!

I got married after high school and my husband and I moved to upstate New York to attend college. My family moved from Cedar Grove during that time. I went back there in the late sixties to visit some old friends, and I asked about the mill. They said that it had been torn down.

Now, what I saw that night wasn't any kind of imaginary thing or figment of my mind, or even an hallucination. I remember that night just as vividly today as I did then, and it still gives me the chills when I talk about it!

What I would like to know from you is whether you have heard of this particular snuff mill before, and who built it and what it was called. We always just called it "the old snuff mill" but I don't know if that was the correct name. I would like to know if anyone else remembers the haunted mill, and whether any of the stories about the man killing his family were true or not.

Any information would be most helpful.

Thanks in advance,

Mrs. G. Hoffman,
Fishkill NY

The Old Snuff Mill, Built in 1800 at Cedar Grove, N.J.

Well, this was not your typical letter (to say the least), so we dug back as far as we could to get to the bottom of this possible snuff-mill murder mystery. (Sounds like the plot of a late night B-movie doesn't it?)

Above is a chroma-tint postcard from around 1910. It is a reproduction of Vernon Royle's 1893 photograph of the mill, apparently still in operation at the time the picture was originally taken.

Phillip Edward Jaeger states in his *History of Cedar Grove* that "According to local legend, it was not possible to walk past the mill without sneezing."

An early map shows it to be "east of the intersection of Little Falls and Bortic Road". This would put it at the present-day site of the Cedar Grove Community Park.

Aside from that, all we know is that the mill was built around 1800 and during the Civil War was temporarily used to manufacture goods for the Union Army.

If anyone out there has more information, please fill us in!

MALE WARDS, ESSEX COUNTY HOSPITAL FOR THE INSANE, CEDAR GROVE, N. J.

The old Essex County Insane Asylum (Above), *located about a mile from the Cedar Grove mill is also supposedly haunted.*

Below: *A jogging trail now marks the spot where the snuff mill once stood.*

More haunted mills?

While researching this article, we were surprised to discover that there are several snuff mills around the world that have a reputation for housing spirits. Here are just a few of them:

The P. Lorillard Snuff Mill - Bronx, New York

THE VENERABLE P. LORILLARD MILL (**LEFT**) CUTS AN IMPOSING FIGURE AGAINST ITS QUAINT OLDE NEW YORK BACKDROP.

Work on the Lorillard Mill originated in 1783, and it was reported to be haunted almost as soon as it was built.

All manner of strange phenomena has been witnessed; including specters, phantoms, poltergeists, strange voices, even a ghostly cat that is said to meow eerily at the stroke of midnight.

Different candidates have been put forth as the possible ghosts that haunt the mill, chief among them being Pierre Lorillard Sr, who was killed by Hessian troops during the American Revolution. The problem with that theory is that P. Lorillard died two years before construction of the mill ever began; why would his ghost haunt a building he never sat foot in?

Regardless of whose ghost actually haunts the grounds, the mill itself stands today. It was put on the National Historic Landmark registry in 1977. It's open for tours to the public, and can be rented out for private ceremonies.

The J & H Wilson Mill, Sheffield England:

Top Mill has long been home to a playful spirit that is said to be the ghost of a young boy who died while under apprenticeship at the mill.

Affectionately named "Eric", witnesses say that the ghost is fond of playing mischievous pranks like blowing out candles and slamming doors and windows. Folks have seen solid objects floating through the air as if being carried by an invisible hand.

The Helme Mill, Helmetta, New Jersey:

The old George Helme Mill has been reported to be haunted since at least the early 1950's, when locals began seeing ominous silhouettes through the windows at night, while no one was inside the factory.

The Helme Mill closed down in 1993 and for many years, its empty shell was a haven for vandals, homeless drunks and drug addicts, partying teenagers, prostitutes, and amateur ghosthunters. Satan worshippers were thought to have practiced ritual animal sacrifice there, as police often found carcasses of cats, dogs, birds, and rodents that had been butchered alive at knifepoint. The residents of Helmetta lobbied heavily for the removal of the factory in order to put an end to the criminal element that the building seemed to attract.

Prior to its demolition, a group of young ghosthunting vandals "investigated" the premises and took several photographs that they later posted online (www. freewebs.com /snuff101). While no spirits manifested themselves on camera, the group did manage to find a couple of creepy things like dead birds and a hand-written note that said "May 19, 1986-Come to basement."

Could it have been written by a ghost attempting to lure an unsuspecting worker to his or her demise? Now that the building is gone, we may never know.

(RIGHT)
THE MILL, AS IT LOOKED JUST PRIOR TO DEMOLITION

(NEXT PAGE)
EERIE SHOT TAKEN FROM WITHIN THE MILL OVERLOOKING THE GROUNDS

QUACKERY!

Featured this month:

Baco-Curo:
A scientific, reliable and harmless cure for the tobacco habit

QUACKERY! is our museum of medicinal mountebanks. Exploring the sometimes laughable, sometimes dangerous world of nicotine addiction "cures" of yesterday and today, it serves to remind us that you shouldn't always believe what you read...

Ah, the good old days, when the cure for nicotine addiction came in pill form.

Actually, there's still a great deal of supposed cure-alls that are readily available over the internet and in health stores. Most are labeled as "dietary" or "all-natural" supplements, since advertising them as medication would require FDA testing and (ahem) double-blind studies that actually *prove* that they work.

These pills usually consist of nothing more than caffeine, ginseng, and whatever other readily available "holistic" or "organic" ingredient the manufacturer can synthesize into pill form. At least in the "golden days" of medicinal quackery, the average consumer was treated to ingredients that *did* produce a noticeable effect.

The active ingredients in most tobacco-cessation medicines were usually opiate-derived. Morphine, heroin, opium, laudanum, as well as plain old alcohol were all commonplace fixtures in headache powders, health tonics, and supplemental pills such as those that purported to cure a myriad of maladies- alcoholism, overeating, impotence, sleep disorders, and of course, nicotine dependence.

It's hard to imagine such a wild west pharmacopoeia in this day and age, but prior to the Harrison Act of 1914, it was commonplace to walk into a general store and buy a pack of Heroin Lozenges to sooth a sore throat as it is now to purchase a bottle of NyQuil. (You could even order a fancy syringe out of the Sears & Roebuck catalog, if you wanted to shoot up in style.)

Once the addictive nature of opiates was discovered, many manufacturers of such products turned to cocaine as a substitute for morphine and heroin. Cocaine was viewed as the new "wonder drug" of the time, and it was a long time before its similarly destructive nature was fully realized. By the time it was made illegal, cocaine had made addicts out of approximately one fifth of the nation.

This brings us to BACO-CURO, a pill that debuted in 1893. Manufactured by the Eureka Chemical and Manufacturing Company of La Crosse, Winsconsin, Baco-Curo's active ingredient was cocaine. Its "all-natural vegetable base" was declared to be safer than other remedies that contained morphine and heroin.

So steady were the sales of Baco-Curo that its chief competitor, "No-To-Bac" out of Chicago, sued Eureka for trademark infringement, owing to the similarity of the two drugs. The case was thrown out of court by the District Judge, who found little in common between the two products.

The printed testimonials of the time raved about Baco-Curo's amazing ability to "energize and revitalize" the temperament of even the most inveterate smoker or chewer. This euphoric buzz was no doubt a result of the cocaine; as anyone who has ever sampled the

Baco-Curo is compounded after the formula and prescription of an eminent German physician, who has prescribed it in his private practice since 1872 to hundreds of cases, without a single failure when directions have been followed.

- From the description on back of tin

Featured Testimonial:

Gentlemen:

For forty years I used tobacco in all its forms. For twenty five years of that time I was a great sufferer from general debility and heart disease.

For fifteen years I tried to quit, but I couldn't. I took various remedies, among them "No-To-Bac", "The Indian Tobacco Antidote", "Double Chloride of Gold", etc. But none of them did me the least bit of good.

Finally, however, I purchased a box of your "Baco-Curo" and it has entirely cured me of the habit in all its forms. I have increased thirty pounds in weight and am relieved from all the various aches and pains of body and mind.

I could write quite a paper on my changed feelings and condition.

Yours respectfully,
Pastor P.H. Marbury
Arkansas

drug could attest to.

It is unknown what happened to all the enthusiastic endorsers of Baco-Curo and its ilk once the government stepped in and outlawed the use of certain ingredients in such over-the-counter remedies. Most manufacturers experimented with substitutes like caffeine, acetanilide (ancestor of acetaminophen), aspirin or even barbiturates. When it was discovered that these replacement drugs lacked the same "kick" that users had come to expect from the older ingredients, the public by and large shunned "quack" cures. Such medicines and tonics were made painfully void and obsolete in the years after the Harrison Act (and the later FDA Act of 1938).

This branch of spurious pharmacology remained fairly dormant until the 1980's, when the popular "New Age" movement ushered in all sorts of "holistic" treatment and therapies for every sort of illness imagined; from cancer cures, to yoga, to meditation for menstrual cramps. It seems that for whatever is wrong with you, there is a pill or a plant that can cure it- *if* you believe it will work. Don't forget, if it's "organic", "holistic", "all-natural" or "homeopathic", it *has* to be genuine, right?

STE

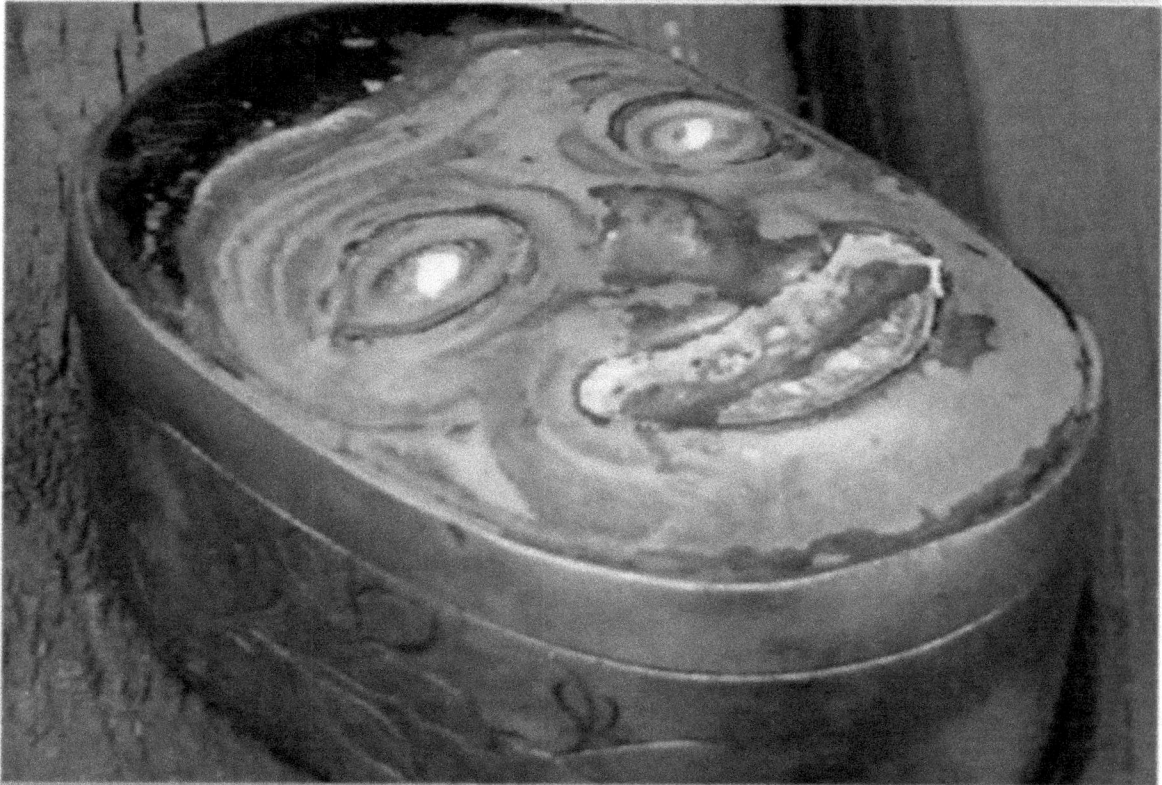

Radioactive Glowing Eye Head

Wow. What a positively ghastly piece of snuff accouterment.

This gruesome imp (looking as though he just stepped out of the fiery pits of Hades) is enough to scare any child away from using snuff. Think about it. If you were six years old and you saw Johnny Diablo's grinning visage sitting across the table, would *you* be tempted to open him up and see what was inside of him? I know I wouldn't. If my grandfather had something like that laying around, I would have had nightmares into adulthood.

This hand-painted relic of the 19th century recently surfaced on Ebay. The seller had no idea where it originated, but we're pretty sure it came straight from hell. If not, that's definitely where it belongs.
It looks kind of like a cross between Pen-nywise the Clown and Slappy the Evil Dummy. As if it wasn't demonic-looking enough already, the painter gave him iridescent green orbs for eyes.

Then to complete the look, he added Linda Blair's blank white pupils that follow you around the room wherever you walk. (If you don't believe us, cut this pic out and hang it on the wall. We dare you.)

STE

57

Meet my friend, Bill Johnson.

We're kicking off Bill's inaugural column with an introduction from a dear friend.

INTERVIEW BY RW HUBBARD

I have known Bill my entire life.

He has been a friend of the family since he and my great-grandfather worked the farms together as small boys. When I initially approached him about this column, the phone call went something like this:

"Hey Bill," I said.

"Yeah?"

"Remember that magazine I told you about? I'm putting it together now, and I was wondering if you wanted to do a column for it."

"What for?" (Typical Bill).

"What do you mean *what for?*"

"I mean, for how much money?"

"Bill," I said, "I can only afford to pay you the same thing I'm paying everyone else."

"How much is that?" he asked.

"Nothing."

He didn't say anything for a minute, but I could hear the sound of him knocking his pipe bowl clean against the mantelpiece.

"Well," he said, "I'll do the column, but I just won't do it as good as I would if you were paying me for it."

"Fair enough," I said.

"What do I have to write about, blackjack or poker?"

"Well, uh... It's a tobacco-themed magazine."

"Oh!" He seemed genuinely surprised. "I thought you said you were doing a card magazine. No wonder you're not paying anyone- who would pay to read about tobacco?"

The preceding exchange pretty much sums Bill up in a nutshell. This is what you should know about him before I turn him loose on an unsuspecting readership:

1. Bill remembers everything, just not always correctly.

He'll remember weddings anniversaries and birthdays, but he forgets which is which. I often get a call on my birthday from Bill, who excitedly wishes me a happy anniversary. On my anniversary, I get a birthday card in the mail with a giftcard for Wal-Mart tucked inside.

2. Bill has been a professional gambler for fifty years.

If you've ever been to Vegas or Atlantic City, chances are you've seen him sitting at the card table. He has been featured in numerous televised tournaments and has co-written three books on the subject, and ghost-written even more. Whenever someone asks him to write, it's usually about gambling. According to Bill, the opportunity to write about something else is a welcome change of pace.

"Well," he said, "I'll do the column, but I just won't do it as good as I would if you were paying me for it."

3. Bill finds it strange that anyone would want to read about snuff and tobacco, and he finds it even stranger that someone would want to publish a magazine about it.

"But Bill," I asked him, "What about rags like *Cigar Aficionado?* That's a pretty big magazine. *Someone* has to be buying it."

"Well yeah," he admitted, "but have you ever *looked* at those cigar books? They've got more articles about golf and ink pens in them than they do about stogies." I couldn't argue there; *Cigar Aficionado's* lack of er, *cigars*, helped give me the impetus to start this magazine. I promised Bill that our magazine would never resort to such backhandedness. The day we run out of articles to run about tobacco is the day that we close up shop.

"But that's my point- they're probably running that material because nobody wants to read about cigars anymore." That brings me to the next item on my list:

4. Bill looks at all sides of an issue and weighs the options.

I think he was trying to gauge whether or not I was trying to ride out a trend (or *start* one, for that matter) before he committed himself to contributing to our folly.

See, Bill Johnson is 80 years old. He's seen a lot of trends come and go, and he has no use for passing fancies. He remembers the early 1990s very well, when those fat, balding businessmen started showing up at the game tables in Vegas with giant cigars hanging out of their mouths, slobbering all over their cards.

Bill doesn't want to be part of a fleeting culture like that. Hell, he still thinks filtered cigarettes are a "gimmick" that won't last. (Having helped to create the world's first popular filtered cigarette, Winston, he may be in a position to pronounce the phenomena as a "fad" even though his prediction may be way off the mark.)

He is concerned that smokeless tobacco like snuff and snus may be just such a fleeting fad. Over in Aspen, he's seen a lot of snowboarding college kids spending daddy's money on Camel snus and Skoal Bandits. "It started about ten years ago," he says. "We had a lot of Swedes coming over to ski there at the resorts, and they all used General snus. Now, the American kids didn't have anything like that here, so they started using Skoal Bandits since they were sort of like portioned snus. "

Despite his apprehension, I've done my best to educate him about the "new" trend in tobacco. We're not all Swedish ski bums or spoiled rich kids. We come from all walks of life- all races, religions, socioeconomic backgrounds- and we like our tobacco. It's not just a prop that we hang out of our mouths to make us look distinguished or powerful- we use it to please ourselves *only* and to impress no one or nothing but our own senses. We love our tobacco.

And so does Bill. That brings us to number five:

Bill Johnson loves tobacco.

In the last eighty years, he has tried every form of tobacco known to man, excepting maybe some Aboriginal strains that never made their way outside of Australia.

He smokes Chesterfield cigarettes daily, although for the last fifty years, he has only smoked three a day. Once in the morning, once after lunch, and one after dinner. He explains his rationing thusly:

"This preacher once told me that smoking was a sin, and I asked him why that was. And he said that any addiction was a sin. So I asked him how to tell if I was addicted or not, and he said that if I smoked a pack a day or more, I was addicted. I smoked probably half a pack a day at that time, and he said I was still addicted. So I asked him, what about a pack a week? And he said that a pack a week probably meant I wasn't addicted. I thought he was full of crap, but I cut down to a pack a week just to be on the safe side."

He still thinks filtered cigarettes are a "gimmick" that won't last.

In addition to his three daily cigarettes, Bill uses nasal snuff, oral snuff, chewing tobacco, cigars, and he smokes a pipe every night before bedtime. "My daddy chewed on a cigar all day long, and at night he smoked a pipe right before he went to bed. He lived to be 99, so I reckon he was doing something right." (I recently gave him a bunch of snus to sample, and he claims that it's not as "queer" as he thought it would be.)

That brings me to number six on my list:

Bill Johnson *knows* tobacco.

Born in a farmhouse in the middle of a large patch of Burley, Bill spent the first fifteen years of his life harvesting tobacco. "I could tell you everything you want to know about growing tobacco- I hated it. It was harder than hard. It made me hate farming for good, and I got away from that as soon as I could."

Bill smoked his first cigarette at age six, his first cigar at age five. He remembers dipping snuff in the second grade and he chewed tobacco all through high school. "It wasn't looked down on like cigarettes were," he remembers. "The teachers really didn't want you smoking. But chewing was OK. You'd go into gym class and after you ran around the track or whatever, the coach would pass around his bag of Mail Pouch or Applejack. There was a bucket in the corner that they called a slop bucket, and that was where you spit your juice."

He finished high school at age 16 and went into the service, eventually fighting in the Korean War and earning a purple heart for his troubles. Upon exiting the military, he came back here and got a job selling hot dogs outside of the RJ Reynolds tobacco factory in North Carolina. "There was this big old guy that would come down four, five times a day and get a hot dog, and we would strike up a conversation. This went on for many months, and one day he formally introduced himself as head of advertising for RJR. He told me that I had a good head for business, and he got me a job in what would now be called the Research and Development department."

While working there, he was part of some of the memorable ad campaigns that came out of the company. "I was there during the *Winston Tastes Good, Like a Cigarette Should* bull sessions. I can say that RJR really went to great lengths to discover what the *people* wanted at that time. The people wanted a filtered cigarette, they wanted it to be on the heavier end of mild, and they wanted it to taste sweet. We came out with Winston, and it was an immediate success. I think that within a few years, it was the best-selling cigarette in the country."

"WINSTON TASTES GOOD, LIKE A CIGARETTE SHOULD." BACK WHEN SMOKING WAS GOOD FOR YOU (1955)

"And Philip Morris, in turn, went to great lengths to make Marlboro a carbon copy of Winston, which it succeeded in. And Marlboro eventually overtook Winston in sales. It wasn't until years later that it came out that Marlboro had way more nicotine than other brands."

Somewhat disillusioned with the behind-the-scenes activities of Big Tobacco, Bill got out of the game before he made any regrets. "When they went with those Flinstone commercials, I was glad to not be a part of that mess anymore."

He tried his hand at various trades, becoming a meatcutter, a copy writer for various newspapers, a radio sportscaster, car salesman; all with varying degrees of success. "When I turned 40, I had sort of a mid-life crisis. I felt that I hadn't really accomplished much in my life, and from there on out, I was only going to do what I enjoyed doing."

Bill enjoyed gambling, and he decided that he was going to be a professional gambler. "In 1966, I made a million dollars playing in Atlantic City. That was when I knew I was doing the Lord's work," he says, only half-jokingly.

And work he did. As a professional gambler, his services were purchased by men and women that had neither the time or the talent to play in casinos. They would put Bill on salary, and give him a line of credit and hope that he won big for him. "I was being paid to do what I loved, and I wasn't in danger of losing any money doing it. That was great when I would occasion-

ally lose, but it's kind of a letdown when you've just won a quarter of a million dollars that you're not going to take home with you."

He was given a monthly column in a New Jersey "sportsbook" (read: gambling guide) and later co-wrote a few books on the subject. He also ghostwrote several articles and guides for some of the "big names" in professional gambling.

"Some of these guys knew how to play, and some big publishing house would give them a million dollars to use their name on the title of a book. You know, *Joe Blow's Guide to Beating the Odds*. They'd say 'Just sign here and don't worry about writing anything, we'll get Bill to ghost it.' It didn't bother me, I made my money regardless. "

Nowadays, Bill is pretty much retired. He still flies up to Atlantic City four times a year, and Las Vegas every two years. The rest of the time he sits around the house watching TV and reading books.

So why did I approach him for our magazine? For one, he's walking proof that moderate tobacco use doesn't seem to harm one's health. "All my physicals check out good. I think like anything, if you overdo it, you're bound to run into problems."

Chewing tobacco has neither rotted his teeth nor given him gum disease, let alone oral cancer. "I have all my original teeth. I've never had any cavities, and my gums haven't receded enough to give me worry. I personally think smokeless tobacco isn't as big a problem as the temperance crowd wants it to be. I mean, I've known fellows that got cancer of the mouth, and they didn't ever use tobacco. But they all drank. Every one of them. But, you don't see giant warning labels on fancy wine bottles saying 'Alcohol is addictive and causes cancer', even though there's more damage caused by alcohol than there ever was with tobacco- excepting for maybe cigarettes."

Incidentally, Bill hasn't touched a drop of booze since 1954. "There's proof positive that alcohol can have a beneficial effect, mainly in its ability to reduce stress. It's the same benefit I receive when smoking a cigar or a pipe before bed, and my way is probably less dangerous." He further offers this advice: "If you've got a lot of stress in your life, take up pipe smoking. But don't overdo it, or it will lose its sheen and become just another habit. Don't inhale it either, or it will become a source of nicotine replenishment. Smoking a pipe is a sacred thing, one not to be abused. It's hard to remain angry when smoking a pipe. And you just plain look smarter with one in your mouth."

"So I recommend putting down the whiskey and picking up a pipe. You won't get depressed smoking a pipe, or have a hangover the next day, or say stupid things to your family or beat your wife and kids when you're in a bad mood. You definitely won't cause an accident on the highway when you've had too much to smoke."

But what *does* Bill use when he needs his "nicotine replenishment"? Snuff. Lots of it. "I like it all. British, German, American- it all has its merits. Some brands I like better in the nose, and some I like better in the lip. It all depends on the brand and cut."

In Bill Johnson, we have an octogenarian in perfect health that uses tobacco in all its forms every day. 'Impossible!' cries the naysayer. 'Tobacco equals death , no exceptions!' Equally disturbing are the ones that warn that just because he's in his eighties, cancerous death may be awaiting him at any second now...

Well, we know better than most of these self-professed "experts". Bill is living proof of that. And he's got a lot to say about the subject. He also suffers fools very badly, so you can bet that there will be a lot of articles about the people that Bill finds foolish.

I'm trying to think of other things you should probably know about Bill. He hates technology, and doesn't own a computer or a cell phone. His typewriter broke down years ago and he has no intention on repairing or replacing it. Everything he writes comes to my desk on loose-leaf notebook paper, inked by fountain pen. "Computers and email- man, that stuff's for squares."

What else? Oh, he refuses to buy anything made in Korea, Germany or Japan. "I'm still here to remember what they did to us during the war. Lots of kids now don't know any better, but I'll be damned if I ever buy Toyota." He makes an exception for German snuff, however, since "Hitler hated tobacco, so a German that used snuff was sort of giving Hitler and the Nazis the finger. At least, that's what I think."

I think that I've pretty much covered all the important parts. I'll let Bill do the rest of the talking from here on out.

— R.W. Hubbard

Notes from the Underground

Bill Johnson

A preachment dear friends,
you are about to receive
on John Barleycorn, Nicotine,
and the temptations of Eve.

My name is Bill Johnson, and I've been invited to write some sort of column for the snuff magazine.

When your publisher got around to asking me about writing, he told me I could write about whatever I pleased. If, for some reason, I run off at the mouth or go off on a tangent, don't take it out on me. Blame your publisher. I warned him.

****

I was thinking back to what I knew about snuffing. Not a whole lot, I suppose, but enough to fill out a few columns here and there.

I remember when I was little, there was a girl that lived next door to us. She was a hell-raiser. You could hear her getting a beating every night for doing something to cause her family grief. She's at the root of what may be my earliest memory regarding snuff.

****

We were in the field one day watching the older folks work. I guess I was about four or five, and she was maybe eight or nine. She kept spitting in the dirt next to the steps. "Ptew." She'd look at me again and then bend over and spit once more. "Ptew."

I guess she finally got tired of me waiting to ask her what she was doing, so she told me. "I'm spitting snuff," she said. "Ptew."

I knew what snuff was, and I knew that it was something that we kids weren't supposed to have. I told you she was a hell-raiser.

"Where'd you get it from?" I asked her.

"My momma buys it for me. Her and my daddy let me do anything I want, even drink corn likker if I want some." I was partly impressed, partly shocked.

64

'If her folks let her do all that stuff, then I wonder what she does to get beat every night?' I pondered.

When dinnertime came and she had gone home, I told my dad about her snuff habit. He got a good chuckle out of it.

"Mary lies real bad, son. She didn't have snuff, I'm sure of it."

"But I saw it, daddy! She was spitting and everything!"

He told me that I got fooled, and I was insulted. He wasn't even there, how did he know?

****

The next day I saw Mary over in her yard, and she waved me over. Our yards were separated by a narrow-wired fence that was probably three feet off the ground. Back then, people didn't build fences for privacy or security; fences were built only to mark property lines.

"Ptew." (She was dipping snuff again.)

I can't remember what happened next, but I know that she did something to make me angry. I think she hit me with a rock. All I know for sure is that I was mad as hell, and I walked up to the back door of their house and I hollered for her mother.

Her mother came out and I told her what her daughter had done. She didn't seem surprised, nor did she make any indication that she would punish her little girl for whatever it was she had done to me.

A BOTTLE OF **GARRET SCOTCH & RAPPEE** WAS A COMMON FIXTURE IN MOST HOMES OF THE ERA.

Mary laughed at me. One of those real mean little girl laughs. "Haw haw."

I decided to go all out. "And... And Mary's been dipping snuff all day and yesterday!"

Aha, now we're getting somewhere. "Is that true?" her mother asked.

"Nuh uh!" she answered.

"Is too!" I replied. "She's got some in her mouth right now!"

Her mother walked over to her and held her hand out under Mary's chin. "Spit it out. Now."

"Ptew."

I could feel my face getting redder than a barn. Instead of snuff, Mary had spit out a mouthful of sunflower seeds.

Her ma told me to go and to

not come over until I could mind my own beeswax. I did as she told me, even though I was so angry I was about to cry.

I learned two things that day; first, never trust what a woman says because it is in their nature to lie; and second, that you should always listen to what your father has to say, because he's probably right.

Ptew.

****

Back then it was customary for girls to use snuff. Cigarettes weren't quite "in" yet on the farms. Younger men chewed tobacco. Middle-aged men smoked cigars. Old men smoked corncob pipes. (Some old men smoked "English" pipes, which is what we called any pipe that wasn't made out of corncob).

Young ladies dipped snuff, and old ladies smoked pipes like their husbands. You never saw a man dipping snuff– if you did, you probably figured he was homosexual. If you did see a man using snuff, he inhaled it off of the back of his hand, or from between his thumb and forefinger. But there wasn't a whole lot of men that took snuff anymore, even then.

The only time I can remember my father using it was when he had run out of chew. "Go get your momma's snuff can off the porch," he'd say, and I would bring it to him and he'd take a great snort and sneeze on the floor. It always made me laugh.

****

So though you never saw men dipping snuff , the ladies had all sorts of ways of taking it. Some would lick the end of a broom straw and dip it in their snuff-box, then put it up in their mouth and chew on it. Some would take a "cavvy stick" and do the same.

(A cavvy stick was a hardened stalk from a tobacco plant that had been heavily sweetened by soaking it in molasses or cara-mel. I'm pretty sure that "cavvy" was short for "cavendish". People made their own cavendish tobacco with all types of things, including sweet elixirs like Hadacol and Dixie Dew.)

Then there was the women that had a little metal snuff spoon that they would lick with their tongue to get moist, then dip it into their snuff container, bring it back up to their mouth, and let it rest against their cheek– spoon and all. Some would just use the spoon to shovel the snuff into their gumline.

Finally, there was the type of woman that didn't need any such accruement. She would just take a pinch and put it in her lower lip. She would repeat this maneuver again and again until she was content with her nicotine dose. Usually the last little bit of powdered snuff that clung to her fingertip was rubbed into the gum. Waste not, want not.

My grandmother was this latter type. Dipping her wet finger in the dirty brown, glass snuff jar,

bringing it up to her mouth, and rubbing it into her upper gum, she would mutter that it "Keeps the cavities away."

****

When I left home and went into the service, I noticed the yankees all dipped snuff. (*Yankees* are what we called all the guys that talked funny. Most of them were actually from the mid-west, and some were even honest-to-goodness northerners.)

Us boys from the south were amazed that *men* were doing such a feminine ritual, but their snuff was a lot different from what we had back home. It was so moist you couldn't inhale it even if you wanted to; it was made to go in your mouth like chewing tobacco. They had strange names like Copenhagen and Key. There was even minty flavored ones like Skoal and Work Mate.

Some of the guys called it "snooze." At least, that's what I thought they called it for the last fifty years. When I started hearing about "snus," I made the connection. The guys that called it that were all from Minnesota and Wisconsin, areas with a heavy Swedish population.

It was awhile before I got around to trying "snooze." But I'll never forget my first time.

****

I was in Korea, fighting that damned war as best as I could. The routine was pretty much the same: march, dig in, wait for some gooks to shoot at you. (That was what we called Koreans back then. I know that the word "gook" is a pretty derogatory term now,

67

but at that time, it was just what we called them. You never heard an officer say anything like 'OK boys, the Koreans are right over that hill.' They'd say something like 'Allright boys- let's climb that hill and kill us some gooks.')

So if you'd been there a few hours and the gooks hadn't started shooting at you, you could grab a ration and smoke a cigarette, or try to shave or clip your toenails. (Most of us didn't shave or clip our toenails.) Inevitably, some guy would get a poker game going

for example, equaled a Camel.

This particular day, I was cleaned out of my cigarette ration. No more for a week. What a miserable week it was going to be, having to bum a smoke all the time.

I went to beg a cigarette off of one guy, and he handed me a can of Copenhagen Snuff. "This here's better than smoking," he said. I took a pinch and put it in my lip, and I handed the can back to him

"Keep it," he said, "I've got a box full." Gee, thanks mister.

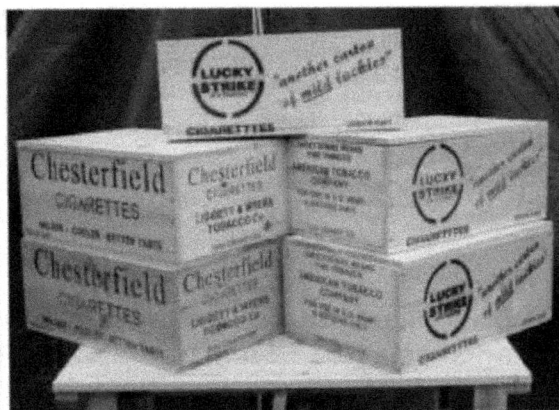

and there'd be a circle of men playing hearts or blackjack. If you wanted to gamble, you played Texas Stud.

The stakes were your cigarette rations. One cigarette equaled a nickel, a whole pack equaled a dollar. 'I raise you a nickel,' you'd say, and then ante up your Camel or Lucky. Some brands were worth less, though. Two Philip Morris's,

Strangely, I liked it. The closest thing to Copenhagen I had ever tried was Maccaboy snuff, which was sort of moist and smelled like gasoline. This Cope stuff was allright. Tasted kind of like barbecue sauce. In a weird way, it reminded me of home.

Right about then, while I was all stretched out in the dirt, lying back tired, and sleepily

We all hunkered down in the trench, waiting for the shooting (or the rain) to stop, whichever came first.

It was a long time before either one ceased.

reminiscing about the rib joint I ate at in Houston the last time I was on leave, some gooks got together and decided it was time to shoot some Americans. Damn it all.

It had started raining, too. We all hunkered down in the trench waiting for the shooting (or the rain) to stop, whichever came first. It was a long time before either one ceased.

****

So that was my first time dipping snuff. Sitting in a mud pit in the middle of Korea, 1951. Cold, wet, tired, miserable, and sick of getting shot at. Wishing I was home, eating pork ribs and smoking cigarettes. God, I wanted a cigarette. But at least I had some snuff.

Ptew.

STE

Bill Johnson can be reached at

Bill Johnson
c/o The Ephemeris
PO Box 287
Spring Lake, NC 28390

Make sure you use large print, because Bill's really old. (Don't tell him I said that.)

There's so many strange items in the world of snuff collectibles that we created the "Creepy Snuff Paraphernalia Award of The Month" section to highlight a choice few. The "green eyed dummy face" box may lose some of its effect when this issue is printed in black & white, but trust me- that thing was unnerving as hell.

****

What to say about Bill Johnson? The man is an octogenarian and has been everywhere and done everything. Bill has at one time or another been a farmer, actor, singer, radio host, soldier, professional gambler, tobacco "drummer" (ad man), and writer, just to name a few things. He's got a story about any subject you can think of, including tobacco. This intro, and the accompanying article, became the best-liked piece in the entire issue, for good reason. Bill is a living legend.

****

"The Snus King" translation had started about a year previously. I initially started translating the book from Swedish to English just for the amusement of a few friends. By the time we began putting this issue together, I had the first two chapters translated and Mick prompted me to put it in the magazine. This opened up a whole new can of worms for us; trying to get permission to serialize a translation of the book for *The Ephemeris*. I spent the next two weeks on the phone with various Swedes following a paper trail that went nowhere. I'm sure that I spoke with at least thirty people trying to get a confirmation from the team behind the original work. To this day, I still don't know who the actual author of *Snus Kungen* is; hence the credit to the Swedish Tobacco Museum who first published the book.

Finally a "higher up" with the organization gave me an off-the-record blessing to translate the work. I made sure that we covered our asses by quoting the "fair use" doctrine. Later on when we were invited to visit the Stockholm Tobacco Museum, we were all told by the staff how much they enjoyed our translation. So I guess that's as official an endorsement as we'll likely ever get.

J.F. Ljunglöf is arguably the most important manufacturer in snuff history, aside from maybe Pierre Lorrilard. His innovations are still in use today, not just in the Swedish Snus industry, but in the way European and American oral and nasal snuffs are presently manufactured. His story needed to be told, and I felt that *Snus Kungen* captured it perfectly. It just needed to be in English! After we're finished with this translation, we have two or three heavily requested foreign-language books on the back burner that will receive the same treatment.

****

"Blackguard of the Month" was a reaction to some of the politicians and pundits who in essence, pissed us off so much that we really had no option but to run a frothing-at-the-mouth rebuttal to their idiotic actions. Henry Waxman, probably one of the most evil politicians that has ever lived, "won" our first Blackguard award. We still hate him.

CONTINUED ON PAGE 84

Snus King:

Ljunglöf's *Ettan* And The History Of Swedish Snus

An Ephemeris Exclusive

Original text by the Swedish Tobacco Museum

In 1999, the Swedish Tobacco Museum of Stockholm published the definitive biography of the man behind the modern snus industry, J.F. Ljunglöf. Creator of Ettan and originator of the steam-pasteurization method of snus production, Ljunglöf was perhaps the single-most important figure in the history of snus.

Readers in English-speaking countries have waited over a decade for a rumored translation that never appeared. Our publisher took it upon himself to Anglicize the text to the best of his ability. We at the *Ephemeris* proudly present a chapter-by-chapter serialization of the book for the benefit of our readership.

A Note On The Translation

This work began as a labor of love that started almost two years ago, when I took a couple of Swedish Language courses in order to better understand some of the old books and flyers I had accumulated over the years.

What started out as a quick translation for a couple of my buddies turned into an expansion of the original work that sought to cover not only the story of J.F. Ljunglöf, but of the entire Swedish snus industry in general.

So a strict reading of the original text side-by-side with my own will reveal a vast difference in the two. Whereas the original text was geared toward a modern Swede familiar with the basic history of Sweden and its snus in mind; much of the information would be unfamiliar to non-Scandinavians and would need a thorough explanation in order to be fully comprehended.

It is in this manner that I have taken great liberties not only with the language, but in some of the historical text as well. For such expansions I relied heavily on Walter Loewe's *Petum Optimum* and Jan Rogozinski's *Smokeless Tobacco in the Western World.* Any errors in the translation should be attributed to myself and none of the original authors.

Finally, I have tried for the last year to receive written clearance from the Svensktobaksmuseet to publish my translation, which we feel clearly falls into U.S. Fair Use guidelines. Although I received blessing from the original editor of the book, written consent was unobtainable due to bureaucratic issues beyond anyone's control.

Therefore I wish to make clear that this work is presented purely for scholastic benefit and purposes of educational research, and all information quoted within is copyrighted by the Swedish Tobacco Museum.   -RWH

Note: this translation will correspond roughly with the layout of the original book, which starts out with the preface below. Sidebars, footnotes, and subheadings will appear either as standalone text or incorporated into the main articles. The chapters will appear chronologically in each issue of the STE until the completion of the translation.

Prologue

"THE CHRISTIANS MET ON THE WAY MANY PEOPLE WHO WERE GOING TO THEIR TOWNS, WOMEN AND MEN, WITH A FIREBRAND IN THE HAND, AND CERTAIN WEEDS WHOSE SMOKE THEY INHALE, WHICH ARE DRY WEEDS STUFFED INTO A CERTAIN LEAF ROLLED INTO THE FORM OF A MUSKET MADE OF PAPER, LIKE THE ONES THE CHILDREN MAKE ON THE DAY OF THE HOLY GHOST; AND BURNING A PART OF IT, FROM THE OTHER PART THEY SUCK OR ABSORB OR ADMIT THE SMOKE WITH BREATHING."
— CHRISTOPHER COLUMBUS, 1492

On Columbus's maiden voyage to the Caribbean, he discovered among the natives the strange mistress of *tobacco*, which the natives smoked, chewed and snuffed. Tobacco spread from Portugal to France, where Ambassador Jean Nicot presented the plant to Catherine De Medici in the form of nasal snuff. The Queen Mother was tormented by migraine headaches, and Nicot's snuff cure worked.

Soon the medication favored by Her Majesty became fashionable to take by the European royal families. So the custom arose to *tabac a pris och snus*- to "take a pinch of snuff".

The new custom spread slowly to Sweden. A land barren of the fine wine and high culture favored by the French aristocracy, the perfumed snuff was a bit of a curiosity to all but the most aristocratic Swedes, who were the only ones able to afford such a luxury. The food of the peasantry was almost exclusively salt-cured, and what little tobacco they were able to procure was salted down the same way. By 1800, a new social custom had replaced the traditional wine and bread dinner- snus and coffee.

It was around that time that the Swedes began tooling the dry snuff of the aristocracy into moist, aromatic oral *snus*. By the end of the century, nearly every man, woman and child in Sweden was consuming it.

Snus was both a remedy for ills and a prevention for disease. Common flavorings were salt, malt, spice, juniper, wine, and syrup.

However, the tobacco grown in Sweden was weak, skinny, and substandard (compared to American tobacco). After harvesting, the stalks were hung up in the barn to cure for up to six months, during the warmest part of the year. The bacterial growth was rampant. In short, snus hardly tasted as good as it does today.

One man set out to change the way snus was made, and his invention was as fresh and modern back then as it still is today, almost two hundred years later.

CHAPTER ONE:

A NOSE FOR QUALITY

"When the men snused, we took the thumb and forefinger of the right hand and spaced them apart about an inch.. Then we took the dose of snus, which we called a "pris" [literally, a "price"]."

- *Frans Petersson*
Born in the 1880's near Urshults Parish.
(People's Life Archives, Lund.)

Wholesaler JF Ljunglöf was a harsh, stern man with a large nose, and he wasn't ashamed to admit it, either. Many people would ask the Snuff King what the secret behind his snus was, and he would proudly point to his bulbous nose and say "here!"

To simply taste the snuff was not enough for him. Day in and day out, year after year, the first thing he did in the morning was call for a sample of yesterday's finished product to be brought to his desk. A pris of snus was scooped up with a silver snuff spoon and snuffed into each nostril. Then he would blow his nose contentedly into his checkered handkerchief. If the snus passed his nasal examination, it was put out for sale that morning.

To be sure, Ljunglöf never intended Ettan to be used under the lip, but to be inhaled in the nose. As shocking as this act may seem today, it was a common (though increasingly less popular) custom of the day.

Ljunglöf's morning examinations became increasingly more strict, and the quality and reputation of Ettan grew considerably. Ljunglöf was obsessed with perfection, and he demanded it in all aspects of his business. This was the way he was raised, and his

perseverance paid off when he inherited the country's leading snuff mill.

Jacob Fredrik

To put it another way, it wouldn't be fair to say that Ljunglöf *inherited* anything, as he had absolutely nothing to his name when he took control of the snus factory, save for empty hands and a net worth of zero dollars. But he had a good, stubborn business sense that landed the name "Ljunglöf" in every man's mouth- literally.

The legendary Stockholm tavern *Clas pa Hornet* housed a small brothel and an even smaller tobacco factory. Thus began Ljunglöf's career in the tobacco industry. In 1813, having reached the age of 18, he left his home and family for good in order to learn all aspects of the trade. Determined to succeed, he traveled to Stockholm with the hope that something would turn up in his favor.

Upon finding employment at the tavern, he received a quick education in tobacco production and accounting. At the age of 24, he was promoted to manager and became a shareholder in the Drottninggatan 81 factory. One of the country's oldest, it dated back to the early 1600s.

Entrepreneurs in Sweden were still under the veil of medieval bureaucracy at the time, and to be able to sell something in a city or a town was considered a rare privilege. The bureaucracy was stingy when it came to granting permits to sell things under your own name, so as to inhibit competition among vendors.

The reasoning behind this policy is somewhat obscure, but it is thought that by restricting the number of merchants selling or manufacturing certain products, there would be less squabble between businessmen; social harmony would then prevail and the bureaucrats would have less paperwork to file . One advantage to this unwritten rule was that if you were lucky enough to be granted such manufacturing rights, you were certain to hold a legal monopoly in your area, thereby making some manufacturers extremely wealthy. A strange mixture of extreme socialism combined with unbridled capitalism, it's a social manner characteristic of Sweden even today.

Nevertheless, Ljunglöf received the necessary permits to sell, and was soon on his way to making his snus a famous brand.

Names and numbers

SILVER BOXES (RIGHT) THAT WERE BROUGHT TO THE "SNUS KING" WITH A SAMPLE OF YESTERDAY'S PRODUCT INSIDE. (FRONT TIN IS STAMPED "NO. 1" AND BACKGROUND TIN IS STAMPED "NO. 2".)

"NO. 1" WAS A COMMON TRADEMARK FOR MOST SNUS FACTORIES, AND IT SIGNIFIED THEIR PREMIUM SNUS. QUALITY GRADUALLY DIMINISHED AMONG THE DESCENDING NUMBERS, WITH "NO. 2" AND "NO. 3" BRANDS BECOMING LESS DESIRABLE.

THIS NUMBERED SYSTEM SURVIVED INTO THE TWENTIETH CENTURY. A GENERAL FORMULA FOR THE NAMING OF THE SNUS WOULD BE AS FOLLOWS: THE NAME OF THE SNUS MAKER, FOLLOWED BY THE LOCATION OF THE FACTORY (OR PLACE WHERE THE SNUS WAS IMPORTED FROM) AND FINALLY BY A QUALITY NUMBER INDICATION.

AMONG ETTAN'S COMPETITION, BLANDINING *NORKOPPINGSNUS* NO.1, LJUNGLOF'S OWN *STOCKHOLM* NO.1, AND LINDHOLM'S *GÖTEBORG RAPÉ* NO.1 WERE ALL POPULAR BRANDS OF THE DAY.

DESPITE THE OFFICIAL NAME OF THE SNUS, THE PUBLIC SIMPLY CALLED THEIR FAVORITE BRANDS BY THEIR POPULAR ABBREVIATIONS, AND LJUNGLÖF'S NO. 1 WAS SOON KNOWN AS JUST "ETTAN". ("ETTAN" IS A SLANG TERM MEANING "NUMBER ONE", THE EQUIVALENT OF THE ENGLISH TERMS "A1" OR "PRIME").

LJUNGLÖF'S NO.2 WAS A LESS EXPENSIVE BRAND THAT FAILED TO SELL ONCE THE POPULARITY OF ETTAN GREW. RECORDS SHOW THAT LJUNGLÖF ALSO MANUFACTURED A "NO. 3" AND "NO. 4" SNUS AT VARIOUS TIMES. "NO. 2" WAS DISCONTINUED BY THE TOBACCO MONOPOLY IN 1916.

J.F. LJUNGLÖF,
CIRCA 1843

In 1822, the name of the factory was officially changed to the Ljunglöf Tobacco Factory. When the original owner died a few years later, Ljunglöf bought all rights to the business from his widow, for the sum of 110,000 dalers. (In today's money, the equivalent of $822,000 USD.)

Not bad for the peasant son of a clergyman.

The firm was thereafter called the *Jac. Fr. Ljunglöf Tobaksfabrik*. The young businessman then married into the wealthy Skeppsbroadeln family, where his father-in-law convinced him to turn the factory's operations over to skilled workers, so that Ljunglöf could manage trade in the lucrative East India Company. Life was good, and Ljunglöf should have been satisfied. Quite simply, he was not.

In Ljunglöf's day, competitors in all sectors copied each other healthily. If a Gothenburg factory had a best seller with a "Göteborg Rapésnus", it was not uncommon for, say, a Noorköping factory to come out with its own version of *Göteborg Rapé*. More often than not, the location listed on the label had nothing in common with the origin of the tobacco used, or its place of manufacture. A

"Göteborg" snus was more likely to have been imported from France, Portugal, Turkey, or another town in Sweden, than it was to have been made in Gothenburg.

It would be an extraordinary feat to make the public become so familiar with your brand that the inevitable copycats that sprang up would be dismissed as cheap imitations. Ljunglöf went to work making Ettan just such a brand.

First though, let us look back at the history of tobacco in Sweden prior to Ljunglöf's era.

Snus as Sustenance: 1611-1799

By Karl XI's time, tobacco use had already ingrained itself into the Swedish military. The cultivation of tobacco was a large economic boon to much of the country. The industry continued to grow into the 1800s.

Nasal snuff use, however, seems to have died out toward the end of the French Revolution. In many parts of Europe, it was encouraged to take up another form of tobacco use (mainly, pipe smoking or cigars) rather than to mimic the snuff habit that was so heavily identified with the French *bourgeois*.

But the heyday of Sweden being a world power ("One third of the power hierarchy", according to Napoleon) was coming to a close. The government encouraged the Swedish populace to start becoming more self-sufficient, and to not rely upon goods imported from other countries, tobacco being no exception. The people turned to their own farmland, and it became customary for most families to grow, cure, and manufacture their own tobacco goods.

From snuff to pipes to chewing to snus - Sweden searches for a tobacco habit to call Her own:

1800-1820

With snuff-taking in decline, chewing tobacco reached the peak of its popularity at the end of the 18th century. Farmer's wives learned how to spin cured tobacco leaves on the same looms that they wove cloth from. These strands were then braided together to form a twisted plug that the farmer could carry with him to the field. The farmer would slice off a bit with his knife as needed and put the rest in his pocket for later.

The dried plug was convenient to carry on one's person, since it didn't attract dust or pocket lint. But back in the house, the farmer was more likely to use a special batch of chewing tobacco that had been moistened in a sweetener such as molasses or caramel. This type of plug was rarely carried outdoors due to its knack for attracting insects and dust with its sticky coating.

At the same time, smoking became common-place to the enlisted men fighting the Thirty Years War. Pipe smoking was considered a good way to for the men to pass the time during the harsh conditions. (In fact, it is said that Russian POWs first introduced cigarette smoking to the Swedes during this engagement).

Smoking was considered a good way to for the men to pass the time during the harsh conditions. (In fact, it is said that Russian POWs first introduced cigarette smoking to the Swedes during this engagement).

Turning Snuff Into Snus

"THE PEOPLE BOUGHT MANUFACTURED GOODS, BUT PLANTED AND CRAFTED TOBACCO AND ITS ACCESSORIES FOR THEIR OWN USE."
-Swedish Historical Record, ca. 1810

"MANY OF THE OLD ALMANACS FEATURED INSTRUCTIONS ON MAKING YOUR OWN SNUFF BOX. THESE WERE FASHIONED OUT OF SUITABLY-SIZED BIRCH BARK, FIVE INCHES LONG ON AVERAGE, AND CARVED BY KNIFE.

THE SNUFF BOXES WERE FILLED WITH DRY TOBACCO, AND THE LIDS WERE OPENED WITH LITTLE RESISTANCE. THE SNUFF WAS TAPPED ONTO THE BACK OF THE HAND. BUT IN THE EARLY 1800S, SNUFF TAKING WAS IN DECLINE AND MANY OF THE OLD BOXES WERE THROWN AWAY OR GIVEN TO CHILDREN TO USE AS TOYS.

NOW, SNUFF WAS MADE INTO SNUS BY TAKING THE DRY SNUFF AND BOILING IT AT MAXIMUM TEMPERATURE UNTIL IT WAS NICE AND THICK. AND THEN ONE TOOK WHATEVER HE PLEASED (SPICE, OR LEAVES FROM OTHER PLANTS) TO BE USED AS A FLAVORING. ONE THAT I LOOKED FORWARD TO WAS A LITTLE BIRCHWOOD ASH FROM THE FIREPLACE.

THEN THEY PUT THE TOBACCO AND FLAVOR INTO A LARGE POT, AND THEY MIXED IT AND MOISTENED IT FOR A COUPLE OF DAYS. THEN, WHEN IT WAS READY, IT WAS PUT INTO A LARGE CLAY POT. THIS WAS HOW THE PEOPLE HAD GOOD SNUS WITHOUT SACRIFICING MUCH MONEY."

--from the memoirs of Jonas Stolts, ca. 1820

(RIGHT) *Early grinder typical of the Swedish peasantry of the 18th and 19th centuries.*

Such mills were used to grind up spice, flour, tobacco and ash.

But smoking a pipe became impractical during the construction of the Göta Canal, where the customary smoke break was not permitted. The men, with their brows wet with sweat and their hands full with work, turned to chewing tobacco.

There was only one catch- the art of spinning plug tobacco was a craft that enlisted men could not replicate in the trenches, and it was quite impractical to steal away to a farmhouse in the middle of the night to weave a twist on the loom. Despite being in such heavy demand, chewing tobacco sales declined from the years 1800-1820.

Since its earliest introduction into Sweden, nasal snuff had a history of oral use by at least a small segment of the population. The practice didn't become widespread, however, until the early 1800s.

Restricted from smoking and unable to procure chewing tobacco, the soldiers and canal builders turned to the only other form of tobacco that they could use while working-snuff. Snuff was both quite affordable and readily available, and it found a welcome use among the men of the time.

Thus, the origin of widespread oral snuff-use can probably be traced to these same lonely men, hunkered down in trenches, cradling a tin of dry Paris Rappee snuff and wishing it was a nice, thick plug of Mother's sweetened chewing tobacco. The soldier no doubt pondered using snuff in this same manner,

Tracking the tobacco trends in Sweden, 1600-2010

Smoking has historically never been as popular in Sweden as it has been in other parts of the world. When tobacco first made it into the country in the 1600s, chewing and snuffing became quite popular, while pipe smoking never reached the heights that it did in neighboring countries.

Between 1650 and 1720, chewing tobacco was the most popular variety, with snuff a distant second and smoking coming in third. From about 1725 until 1800, snuff became more predominant, eventually eclipsing chewing tobacco in sales during the period between 1810 and 1820. (Smoking still remained in third place, trailing behind smokeless tobacco).

1800-1820 saw smoking becoming slightly more in vogue, and in 1820 it was just as popular as snuff, with chewing tobacco now moving into third place. But by 1830, snuff had evolved into snus and was outselling both chewing and smoking tobacco.

Snus sales increased every year until its peak in 1918, where it accounted for roughly 75% of the total tobacco consumed in Sweden until around 1930.

From 1930-1949, snus use was still dominant, although it was losing ground to cigarettes every year. By 1950, cigarettes were outselling snus for the first time, a trend that continued into the 1960s.

By 1970, smoking began its gradual decline while snus use started a steady incline. This trend continued into 2004, when snus once again became the most popular method of taking tobacco in Sweden.

and an experiment took place. "A little dry," he may have said to himself, "but not bad at all!"

Just like the First World War taught the west how to smoke cigarettes, the Thirty Years War taught Sweden how to use snus. The soldiers brought their snuff habits home with them, and they found a public eager to try the "new" way of taking snuff.

Folks wanted a tobacco product that was easy to make, convenient to use, and not dependent on the natural flavor of the weak tobacco that they grew at home. Something that could be easily ground down in regular flour grinders, or in the same mills that they used to grind up rye and barley. Something that they could flavor with the common ingredients that they had laying around the house.

This was the period in which snus use became really widespread, and it appealed to the lowliest, callous-handed blue collared worker to the stiffest starched-white collared businessman.

STE

Continued next issue: The Birth of Ettan!

THE DANGEROUS CHEWING PLUG

West Indian leaf was popular at that time, and it was all cooked with something called "tobacco sauce". The men would pull it out of their pocket, twist it down the middle, and put it in their mouths.

Tobacco chewers stood out from the other men on the street, because the chewing plug would stick out of their jaws and make them look like they had a large, lumpy potato in their mouth.

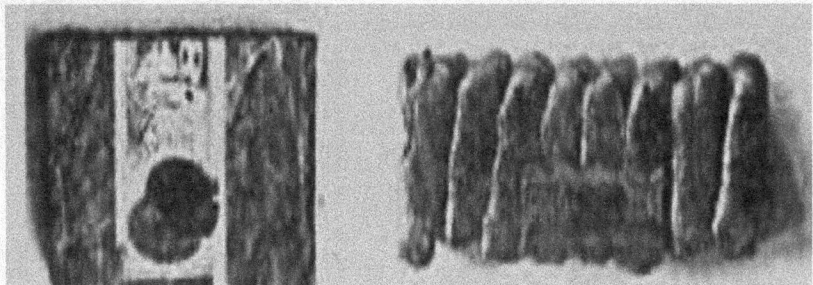

FLAT PACKAGED SPUN TOBACCO (LEFT) AND BRAIDED PLUG "TWIST" OR "TUGTOBAK" (RIGHT).

(PHOTO: J. ROGOZINSKI)

The worst was when they took the plug out, which never happened unless it was time for dinner. The plug would be far back in the jaw, close to the ear, and it would take two hands to remove it from the mouth. It was a sight to see!

If such a plug was thrown away in the road when it was cold out, it would freeze up and become a dangerous obstacle. Once, a worker from Småland came running down the street with a load of wood in his hands, and he slipped on the frozen tobacco.

Had that happened now in the present time, the government would no doubt quickly ban all chewing tobacco.

-AUGUST HOLMBERG, RECALLING HIS YOUTH IN THE EARLY 1800's

ASARUM, SWEDEN
FOLKLORE ARCHIVES, LUND UNIVERSITY

BLACKGUARD OF THE MONTH:

Rep. Henry Waxman

Henry Waxman embodies everything that is wrong with American politics today.

When he's not busy portraying Gollum in the *Lord of the Rings* Trilogy or doubling for Lon Chaney in the original *Phantom of the Opera*, he's busy heading up kangaroo courts and slamming his gavel in childish outbursts of authoritative ignominy. Perhaps the 35 years he has spent serving in the House of Representatives have given him some sort of feeling of entitlement?

The genius behind the mindbending travesty of federal abuse that is the Kennedy-Waxman Tobacco Control Act, Waxman made the USA the laughingstock of European countries that are not used to see-ing such Draconian nannywagging occur in the Land of the Free. While his unconstitutional bastard hodgepodge of lies and misinformation claims to be "for the children," its main directives seems to be to keep cigarettes legal (just more expensive); to ban safer tobacco alternatives like snus, smokeless tobacco and E-cigs; to help Philip Morris gain more marketshare; and most importantly, to give the federal government more power than it was ever meant to have. And just like Tolkien's Gollum, this hog-nosed hobbit is fiercely protective of his "precious" House seat- to the point that many of his colleagues question his reason and sanity.

Henry Waxman is typical of all of the

WAXMAN SNARLS AT AN AT&T EXEC WHO DARED TO QUESTION HIS AUTHORITAH.

greedy Washington swindling crook. He wants an extremely large government that has absolute authority in all matters, civil and private. He wants higher taxes to fund useless programs that benefit his special interests. He lies and bends the truth to get his way, and throws a temper tantrum when he doesn't get it.

He absolutely loathes personal freedom, and wishes to strip it from each and every American citizen systematically and deliberately.

Remember that this November. STE

79

The Connoisseur (1754)

Beginning on January 31, 1754 and running until September 30, 1756, **The Connoisseur** was a satirical British newspaper. Appearing every week for its two-year lifespan, **The Connoisseur** was a parody of the more well-known "society" weekly, **The World.**

The World was published by Edward Moore, playwright and hobnobberer to the London uppercrust of the Georgian Era. Sort of an Eighteenth century Perez Hilton, Moore made sure that his periodical contained plenty of articles that would appeal to the wealthy socialites that he attempted to befriend. This material ranged from the mundane ("Should a Gentleman discuss the political amongst mixed Companies?") to the salacious (muck-raking celebrity gossip).

The Connoisseur mocked the ritzy tone of such publications. The brainchild of satirists George Colman and Bonnell Thornton, **The Connoisseur** mainly consisted of fictitious correspondence between "readers" and the equally fictitious Editor-In-Chief, "Mr. Town".

A typical exchange would begin with some stuffy prude expressing her displeasure at art exhibits that featured "tasteless" works of art like nude statues or erotic paintings. "Mr. Town" would then suggest to the letter-writer that she should train one of her menservants to carry a bundle of cloth on his person so that he may clothe said statue before its lewdness could offend the Lady.

The Connoisseur was perhaps ahead of its time. Though it sold well, the authors' grew bored with the format and pulled the plug less than three years into the magazine's run. The entire series was later reprinted in two volumes under the title **The Connoisseur by Mr. Town, Critic, and Censor-General**. (Subsequent editions spanned three and four volumes). The reprints made the work even more popular than it was while it was fresh, a phenomenon attributed to later generations being more appreciative of satire than their predecessors., (especially when said parody was aimed squarely at the bourgeois).

In this selection, a "reader" bemoans the filthy habit of snuff-taking that had spread from the "savage nations" all the way to London's gentry. It's a hilarious indictment of the anti-tobacco crowd of the era (in fact, with updated vernacular, it could very well be a modern letter written to some tut-tutting periodical like *Reader's Digest* or *Good Housekeeping.*

Presented for your perusal, an excerpted passage from Issue 32 of *The Connoisseur*, Thursday September 5th, 1754.

5 September 1754.
Musings, et; al

Emuncta Naris- **Hor.**

A plain blunt fellow, who, like scented beaux, With vile pulvilio ne'er begrim'd his nose.

TO MR. TOWN.

Sir,

I know not whether you yourself are addicted to a filthy practice, which is frequent among all ranks of people, though detestable even among the lowest. The practice I mean is that of snuff-taking: which I cannot help regarding as a national plague, that, like another epidemical distemper, has taken hold of our noses. You authors may perhaps claim it as a privilege, since snuff is supposed by you to whet the invention, and every one is not possessed of Bays's admirable receipt, the "Spirit of Brains" -but give me leave to tell you, that snuff should no more be administered in public, than Major's medicinal composition at four-pence a pinch[1], or any other dose of physic.

I know not why people should be allowed to annoy their friends and acquaintance by smearing their noses with a dirty powder, any more than in using an eye-water, or rubbing their teeth with a dentifrice.

If a stranger to this nasty custom was to observe almost every one drawing out his pouncet box, and ever and anon giving it to his nose, he would be led to conclude, that we were no better than a nation of Hottentots[2]; and that every one was obliged to cram his nostrils with a quantity of scented dirt to fence them from the disagreeable effluvia of the rest of the company. It might not be absurd in such a stranger to imagine, that the person conversing with took it, for the same reason that another might press his nostrils together between his finger and thumb, to exclude an ill smell.

It is customary among those polite people the Dutch to carry with them everywhere their short dingy pipes, and smoke and spit about a room even in the presence of ladies. This piece of good breeding, however ridiculous it may seem, is surely not more offensive to good manners than the practice of snuff taking. A very Dutchman would think it odd, that a people who pretend to politeness, should be continually snuffing up a parcel of tobacco-dust; nor can I help laughing, when I see a man every minute stealing out a dirty muckender[3], then sneaking it in again, as much ashamed of his pocket companion, as he would be to carry a dishclout about him.

It is, indeed, impossible to go into any large company without being disturbed by this abominable practice. The church and the playhouse continually echo with this music of the nose, and in every corner you may hear them in concert snuffling, sneezing, hawking and grunting like a drove of hogs. The most pathetic speech in a tragedy has been interrupted by the blowing of noses in the front and side boxes ; and I have known a whole congregation suddenly raised from their knees in the middle of a prayer by the violent coughing of an old lady, who has been almostly

[1] *"Major's medicinal composition " was a laxative suppository.*

[2] *"Polite" derogatory term for African natives*

[3] *A handkerchief*

choked by a pinch of snuff in giving vent to an ejaculation. A celebrated actor has spoiled his voice by this absurd treatment of his nose, which has made his articulation as dull and drowsy as the hum of a bag-pipe; and the parson of our parish is often forced to break off in the- middle of a period, to snort behind his white handkerchief.

Is it not a wonder, Mr. Town, that snuff, which is certainly an enemy to dress, should yet gain admittance among those, who have no other merit than their clothes? I am not to be told, that your men of fashion take snuff only to display a white hand perhaps[1], or the brilliancy of a diamond ring- and I am confident, that numbers would never have defiled themselves with the use of snuff, had they not been seduced by the charms of a fashionable box. The man of taste takes his Strasburg veritable tabac from a right Paris paper-box; and the pretty fellow uses an enameled box lined in the inside with polished metal, that by often opening it, he may have the opportunity of stealing a glance at his own sweet person, reflected in the lid of it.

Though I abhor snuff taking myself, and would as soon be smothered in a cloud raised by smoking tobacco, as I would willingly suffer the least atom of it to tickle my nose, yet am I exposed to many disgusting inconveniences from the use of it by others. Sometimes I am choked by drawing in with my breath some of the finest particles together with the air; and I am frequently set to sneezing by the odorous effluvia arising from the boxes that surround me. But it is not only my sense of smelling that is offended; you will stare when I tell you, that I am forced to taste, and even to eat and drink this abominable snuff.

If I drink tea with a certain lady, I generally perceive what escapes from her fingers swimming at the top of my cup; but it is always attributed to the foulness of the milk or dross of the sugar. I never dine at a particular friend's house, but I am sure to have as much rappee as pepper with my turnips ; nor can i drink my table-beer out of the same mug with him, for fear of coughing from his snuff, if not the liquor, going the wrong way.

Such eternal snuff takers as my friend, should, I think, at meal times, have a screen flapping down over the nose and mouth, under which they might convey their food, as you may have seen at the masquerade; or at least they should be separated from the rest of the company, and placed by themselves at the side table, like the children.

This practice of snuff taking, however inexcusable in the men, is still more abominable in the other sex. Neatness and cleanliness ought to be always cultivated among the women; but how can any female appear tolerably clean, who so industriously bedaubs herself with snuff? I have with pain observed the snow-white surface of an handkerchief or apron sullied with the scatterings from the snuff-box; and whenever I see a lady thus besmeared with Scotch or Havannah, I consider her as no cleanlier than the kitchen wench scouring her brasses, and begrimed with brickdust and fuller's earth. Housewifely accomplishments are at present seldom required in a well-bred woman- or else I should little expect to find a wife in the least notable, who keeps up such a constant correspondence between her fingers and nose; nor, indeed would any one think her hands at all fit to be employed in making a pudding.

It should be remembered by the younger part of your fair readers, Mr. Town, that snuff is an implacable enemy to the complexion, which in time is sure to take a tinge from it: they should therefore be as cautious of acquiring a sallow hue from this bane of a fair skin, as of being tanned or freckled by exposing their delicate faces to the scorching rays of the sun. Besides, as the nose has been always reckoned a principal ornament of the face, they should be as careful to preserve the beauty of it as of any other feature, and not suffer it to be undermined or bloated by so pernicious an application as snuff taking. For my own part, I should as soon admire a celebrated toast with no nose at all, as to see it prostituted to so vile a purpose. They should also consider, that the nose is situated very near the lips : and what relish can a lover find in the honey of the latter, if at the same time he is obliged to come into close contact with the dirt and rubbish of the former? Rather than snuff taking should prevail among the ladies, I could wish it were the fashion for them to wear rings in their noses, like the savage nations; nay, I would even carry it still farther, and oblige those pretty females, who could be still slaves to snuff, to have their nostrils bored through as to bear rolls of pigtail bobbing over their upper lips.

We cannot otherwise account for this new fashion

1 "Displaying a white hand" in public demonstrated that you were wealthy enough to not have to work for a living.

Coming Next Issue

Ljunglöf: Snus King Part II

The Byfield Snuff Mill

Herbal Snuff

Legal Weed

New Snuffbox Column

Interviews

... and much, much more !

some of the essays that we've reprinted are available via google books or other internet sources, we work only from the original texts that are stored in our libraries. It's our way of ensuring that these works never fade from print and can be shared with a wider audience.

We're working our way backwards for the most part, reprinting the oldest, most degraded works first before they completely disintegrate. In the case of *The Connoisseur*, which ran in this issue, the 255 year old newsprint crumbled into dust as we attempted to scan it. Thankfully we were able to use a different version from Project Gutenburg to compare ours against and thus the complete, unexpurgated text was in print again for the first time since 1754.

****

When we came back and did the reprint, news had just broken about the USA's capture of Osama Bin Laden. We had an empty space to fill on one page, so I wrote a short piece about helping us "catch Bin Laden by May 2nd," which was the date that he was assassinated. For new readers unaware that this was a Second Edition printing, it would appear that we had accurately predicted the raid on Bin Laden's compound a year before it happened.

Unfortunately very few people got the joke, and we received a lot of letters like "what, you guys think 9/11 was funny?" or "You leftist/hippy/commie scum don't realize that without the War on Terror we would have never caught Bin Laden?" I was just trying to make a humorous comment about the small business taxes that Lucien Publishing was struggling to pay at the time, while pretending we had the ability to foresee the future. I guess it just wasn't funny...

****

The same thing happened with the back cover to the first printing, which was a parody of the "quality statement" found on the reverse side of Camel non-filter packs. To justify the higher price of regular Camels, RJR has always featured the following bit of nonsense on the back of the pack:

Don't look for premiums or coupons, as the cost of the tobaccos blended in Camel
Cigarettes prohibits the use of them.

The fact that they still print this message today is pretty funny, considering what we now know about RJR and Camel history. (When Camel was first introduced, it was comprised solely of Prince Albert pipe tobacco rolled into a white cylinder, not even marginally an "expensive" blend. By the late 50's, Camel was the first cigarette to employ "recon" tobacco, remanufactured tobacco scraps that could hardly be considered luxurious. The list can keep going, but this is supposed to be about the back cover of Volume One, not Camel cigarettes...)

Within days we received letters and emails about the back cover. "How can you put a price on information?" "So you're saying that you're going to jack up the cover price every month because the information is so priceless?" "You're not going to give discounts when you order a ten-year subscription?" One letter writer even called us "arrogant pricks" for the message we printed.

The response to the back cover was so negative that I had to issue a retraction on our blog and explain the source of our "joke" that apparently nobody understood. To this day, I think it has cost us customers who never purchased another issue past our first one, since their fears were justified when the cover price to our second issue jumped an astonishing 3.00.

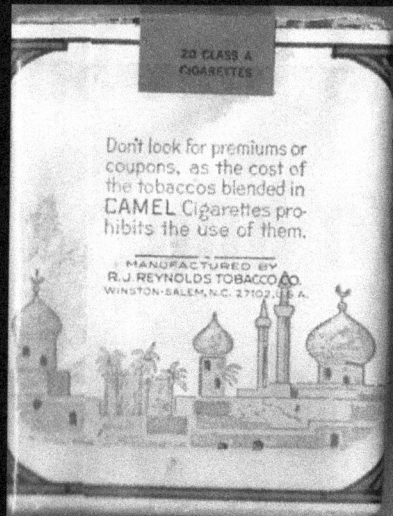

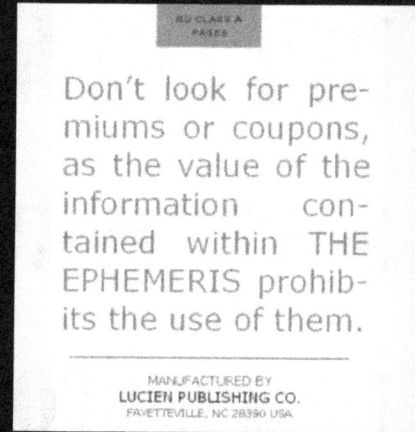

The Camel Pack (left) and our parody (above).

What a lot of folks don't know was that the first issue was *supposed* to retail for about 8.00. We lost money on each copy of the first printing we sold. The cost of printing per issue was well above 7.00, but when I picked up the pitiful results from our local print shops, I couldn't in clear conscious sell them for even what we paid for them. So I decided that we'd mark them down to 5.52, which would be a special "introductory" price and people wouldn't feel quite so ripped off at getting a magazine that looked like it was printed by a bunch of five year olds and stapled together by alcoholics with trembling DT hands. We were betting on the content surpassing the print quality, and I think for the most part the gamble paid off. But believe it or not, two years later Lucien Publishing is *still* trying to recoup the loss that went into our disastrous first printings.

****

One joke that did pay off was the "Bill Lee" ad campaign that has been a regular part of *The Ephemeris* since our first issue. Our goal was to create an ad that looked like it came from a mid-to-late sixties *Look* Magazine or *Playboy*. If you've ever seen the cigarette ads from that era, you'll probably recognize the premise: Joe McEveryman is a normal, hardworking lumberjack that tells it like it is and eschews the fancy girly cigarettes that everyone else smokes. Be a real man, and smoke the same cigarettes as Joe, whether they be Camel, Marlboro or Winston.

Over time our ads have become less straightforward and more ridiculous, much like the rest of our content. But many readers have told us that the very first thing they do when they buy their copy of the STE is flip to the back and check out the latest "_____ *is a snuff taker, and the Ephemeris is his magazine*" ad. This sits just fine with me. When I was a kid, the first thing I did when I brought home a *Mad Magazine* was flip to the back cover and do the Al Jaffee fold-in. Good times...

Bill Lee has just spent the last seventy-two hours underground.

He wasn't down there for fun. He was down there earning a living, the only way he knows how. And tonight, he's going to do it all over again.

Because Bill is a coal miner. And his only companion twelve miles below the earth is his snuffbox. And it's the only thing waiting for him when he gets home.

Bill Lee is a snuff taker.

The Ephemeris is his magazine.

Reserve your copy of *The Snuff Taker's Ephemeris* today at www.snuffmagazine.org.

The "Honest Snuff" ad was chosen to serve as our inside back cover, basically because it happened to be on my desk when I was looking for something to fill up that blank space. Due to a printing error, it never actually ended up in the first edition at all. Then when we did the second printing, the Camel parody ended up on the inside back cover, so the Honest ad was once again nixed at the last minute. (The new back cover was a simple "STE" logo which we use now as the final printed page in each new issue, including this reprint.) Finally, with our third edition, the Honest ad can finally see the light of day.

****

Getting the first issue into the hands of the people was our greatest challenge. We had no distributor, but we somehow managed to get 5,000 copies into tobacco stores and independent bookshops simply by calling the store manager and pitching our book to them, or by walking in with a sample copy and a business card and saying "give us a call if you want to sell our magazine." Our biggest audiences were in Virginia, North Carolina, South Carolina, Ohio and Texas mainly because these were the areas that Mick, Micah and I pounded the pavement trying to drum up interest.

The remaining copies were sold over the internet, also by word of mouth stirred up on the tobacco forums and a couple of press releases. Our pre-order numbers were HUGE... so much so that we ran out of regular copies to sell within a week. e were expecting roughly half of our retailer copies to end up being returned to us for credit, but to our surprise, we didn't receive a single return. This left a lot of readers scouring eBay and Amazon trying to locate a copy. Some of this momentum carried over to our second issue, which also sold out pretty quickly in its first run. The very first thing we did after receiving the net profits from Volume II was to use it to reprint Volume I, and over time that printing too sold out.

After that, things were a blur. The tobacco companies that previously refused to buy ad space from us were suddenly contacting us wanting to know our rates. We were being wined and dined by snuff manufacturers who were flying us all over the world to sample their latest wares. I was invited to speak at publisher's conventions that I had never heard of and wondered how they had heard of me. The buzz had spread like wildfire within the independent publishing company. We were mentioned in magazines like *Publisher's Weekly* under articles such as "turning your fanzine into a prozine" and "mass scale microprinting." But, even with all of the head-swelling applause, Diamond Distributors refused (and *still* refuses) to carry our book and we couldn't find a decent printer to save our lives. We were stuck basically selling the magazine door-to-door and relying on the grassroots community for free publicity, which was the only kind we could afford.

The hard work would eventually pay off, and though The Snuff Taker's Ephemeris is still not a household name, our bookazine is available all over the world to pretty much anyone who wants it. If this is your first time reading Volume One, or your fiftieth, we still hope you enjoyed reading it as much as we enjoyed putting it together.

RW Hubbard
Bangor, Maine
November 11th, 2012

HONEST SNUFF

It is absolutely Pure.

It has <u>no artificial</u> flavor.

It has <u>no</u> moisture.

It is the very essence of Tobacco.

It takes 100 lbs. of the best heavy bodied Leaf Tobacco to make 75 lbs. Honest Snuff.

In Buying HONEST SNUFF you get no casing, no Sweetening, no Moisture.

HONEST SNUFF needs no artificial flavoring to make it pleasing to the taste, because it is made of the strongest and best Tobacco. The natural flavor of the tobacco is developed by a process that eliminates all rankness and moisture.

Consumers of Honest Snuff get the cleanest and purest Tobacco and greater value than in any other form in which Tobacco is used.

THE PROOF.

The following figures prove conclusively that consumers recognize these facts:

They chewed 569,511 lbs. Honest Snuff in 1900
" " 1,400,277 " " " " 1910

This ratio of increase continues, which is due to the growing knowledge among men that <u>HONEST SNUFF IS A MAN'S CHEW.</u>

HONEST SNUFF IS REFINED TOBACCO

AFTERWORD

MICAH D. RIMEL

So there you have it folks.

What you have just read constitutes the earliest incarnation of the STE, our smokeless-themed literary baby. When issue one was first put out it was accompanied by a host of differences; it was much smaller and in a cute (really the only way to describe it, I checked) digest size, like *Asimov's* or *Ellery Queen.* The binding had much to be desired in the way of professional appearance thanks to scurrilous printers but the text was in full color and overall was still a beauty to behold.

Since that first issue back in 2010 we have metamorphosed as individuals both personally and professionally. STE is no longer a small magazine intended mainly to amuse ourselves and attempt to spread the news about snuff, snus, smokeless tobacco, pipes and cigars to whatever audience was waiting. *You* were waiting, dear reader. *You* were there, hungry for what we had to bring to the table and so, two years later, we're still bringing it. We appreciate your support, then and now, and promise to keep bringing the very best in content for ages to come.

So raise a pinch, a pouch, a pull, a portion, a puro or a pipe and toast the issue that brought it all about. Here's to you, Dear Reader, and to Volume One, the whimsical paper place where all the magic began…

Your friend (and mine)

Micah Rimel

Remembering Tom Dunn

Rob Hubbard

To me, the greatest tobacco magazine in the world will always be The Pipe Smoker's Ephemeris. *It was a one-man operation put out by an eccentric, but likable fellow named Tom Dunn whom I was lucky enough to strike up a short friendship via correspondence with in my late teen years.*

TPSE was a hodgepodge pastiche of all things tobacciana; someone looking for a quick read or philosophical "depth" to the material was out of luck. Each issue was like Tom walking you through his collection of tobacco paraphernalia and telling you an interesting story behind it.

Unfortunately Tom died a few years before he could witness the birth of The Snuff Taker's Ephemeris, *named in his honor. Sure, we could have gone with a snazzier, easier-to-pronounce title that would sell a million copies per issue, but I figured if "Ephemeris" was good enough for Tom, then it was good enough for our sleazy little rag.*

The following article was written for Snuscentral.com in November 2010 and I always felt a bit sad about not featuring more about Tom in our inaugural issue, so hopefully this will make amends for my past error. Big thanks to Larry Waters for letting me reprint it here in a slightly expanded form.

As some of you may have heard, Mick and I have entered the publishing business with The Snuff Taker's Ephemeris; a bi-monthly periodical devoted to all things snus and snuff. I wanted to share with SnusCENTRAL one of the many roads that lead me to want to do a book on tobacco. It would be a crime to omit the name of Tom Dunn from the story. This essay is dedicated to the memory of Tom Dunn, 1938-2005.

Most people remember Tom as the founder and publisher of *The Pipe Smoker's Ephemeris*, which he put out regularly from 1965 until his death of stomach cancer in 2005. TPSE, as it was more commonly known by its readers, was the single best tobacco-related periodical ever concocted. Tom never made much off of his magazine- in fact, he probably didn't even break even; there was no cover price most of the time and his Ephemeris was financed exclusively by reader donations and second, third and fourth mortgages on the Dunn home.

TPSE was a word-of-mouth publication, meaning that in the pre-internet days there was really no way of knowing about the book unless you had a savvy tobacconist that would tip you in on the 'secret' magazine. Or maybe you would discover it by an off-the-cuff mention in a "big" tobacco magazine like *Cigar Aficionado*. Wherever you got your first lead, it usually followed with a 411 call to New York in hopes of finding the address of a guy named Tom Dunn in College Point. If you were a Type A person, you would probably just call him (his number was always listed) or if you were a Type B person (like me), you would write him a letter asking for a couple of back issues. If you were a decent person, you'd stuff a couple of five dollar bills in the envelope too. (This would guarantee that you'd end up on the mailing list- a coveted spot if there ever was one).

Tom was first and foremost a historian. A walking encyclopedia of everything tobacco-related, Tom probably had a copy of every book, newspaper article, newsletter, magazine essay, sales bill, catalog

and radio/television special ever produced regarding the subject of tobacco. His home became a sort of a mini-museum housing his archives.

After his death, it was discovered that he had almost fifty filing cabinets full of tobacco-related print material, with each cabinet devoted to its own subject. Every cabinet drawer was numbered, and each number was indexed in a journal. If you wrote to Tom with a question regarding availability of a certain blend of tobacco, he would dutifully pull out the journal and find the right cabinet- Tobacco Sellers (English) catalogs, modern- Cabinet 36. And within a day or two, you'd get a response in the mail telling you exactly what he knew about your inquiry. Tom was the human tobacco search engine. Which is ironic, in that Tom shunned computers. He didn't even own one until very late in his life (and even then he had no internet connection.) Right up to the end, TPSE was produced entirely by hand, Tom banging away on his typewriter and then manually cutting and pasting everything into its proper place before driving 200 miles round-trip to his printer in Pennsylvania. A week later he would make the drive again to pick up the finished product, come home and stick it in an envelope, and hand address it to each subscriber on his mailing list, along with whatever personal correspondence he may have chosen to include.

(You may notice that we often do the same thing with STE copies purchased from our website. Usually one of our interns fills out the customer's name and address by hand instead of printing it out onto an Avery label. Even though it takes longer to do it this way and requires manual labor, I feel like it's one way of keeping the "personal" touch to our magazine. We can also claim to be "green" and eco-friendly by not wasting excess paper!)

I first discovered TPSE in a local tobacconist's shop. Even though I was already smoking cigarettes (which I was too young for) and had tried everything from dip to snuff to chew (I was a really bad boy), pipe smoking was something I attempted in the past but never could get the hang of. But I always salivated at the aromas and fancy pipes in this particular shop. I went there at least once a week, when my brother would go in to buy his usual box of Robt. Burns cigars.

One of these visits, I happened to see my first copy of TPSE, which cost me a cool three bucks if I remember correctly. (Tom would send a stack to certain retailers, who reimbursed him with pipes or bulk tobacco). The cover was out of this world- black and white, illustrated and smacking of the indie comix I grew up with. It stood out so prominently on a counter full of the "prestige" and colorful cigar rags you usually see. Flipping through it, I saw an in-depth Sherlock Holmes article and I was instantly sold. I read it cover to cover until it was in tatters.

I soon found myself intrigued with the pipe and cigar talk inside. I immediately subscribed and went back to the smoke shop armed with a knowledge of Dunhill and Mac Baren tobacco blends that I needed to try (unfortunately, Carter Hall was about as fancy a tobacco as you could get in that particular store). I also got my first pipe, a standard beginner's Missouri Meerschaum corn cob that I still use to this day. (Remember, this was back when older looking teenagers could pretty much buy anything they wanted- porn, booze, smokes- without being asked for ID. I shudder to think of how many laws I broke during that time period.)

Coming from a tobacco-industry background myself, I started writing to Tom about different aspects of the trade, and to my surprise he always wrote back. I even submitted an article to him about the French cigarette industry during World War II, which he loved but refused to print because I wasn't "old enough" yet. That really rubbed me the wrong way and I canceled my subscription the next day. I still, for the life of me, don't really know quite what happened there, but I didn't read TPSE again until about 2001, when a stray copy was given to me at a tobacco convention.

By 2003 I was a subscriber again, and renewed my correspondence with Tom. The old flap over the article was long forgotten by the both of us, and Tom sent me much material regarding snuff and smokeless tobacco, a new interest of mine. There was very little information about snuff and snus on the internet in those days, so the material I received was invaluable. Though he was (of course) a pipe smoker first, he always carried a tin of his own personal blend of Gawith and Hoggarth snuff for those rare occasions when he couldn't smoke his pipe. He (rather sheepishly) admitted to enjoying the occasional plug of chew while working outside.

Tom Dunn was also the first person I ever heard mention Swedish snus, a type of tobacco he was fascinated with ever since reading an article about it in a 1980 issue of The Smithsonian. The following is from a letter he sent me in late 2004:

"... but if you're going to chew snuff, you would be hard pressed to find a better example than the Swedish variety. [A Swedish member of his pipe club] sends me a brand called "Rallarsnus" and "Generalsnus" which are both very good. Unlike American or English chew, you do not have to swallow the expectoration, which is intriguing from an American standpoint to say the least!"

When RJR rolled out Camel snus a couple of years later, I was living in Austin, which was basically one of the only two cities in the US where you could get the original Camel snus. I sent a can to Tom to get his opinion on how it compared to the Swedish brands. I never received a reply though, and it wasn't until later I heard that Tom had passed away shortly before Christmas. I sent my regards to his family, knowing the tobacco world had lost a true legend.

Five years later, I found myself (due to a bizarre series of coincidence that could probably warrant its own article) the proud owner of the contents of **Cabinet 19**, the Smokeless Tobacco Archives of Tom Dunn. The files contained newspaper and magazine articles about snuff dating back to 1955, along with stacks and stacks of correspondence to snuff makers and sellers from all over the world. Everything you always wanted to know about smokeless tobacco, stacked in no particular order and covering the history of snuff first-hand for a half a century. It took me weeks to go through everything, and what I've ended up with is a treasure trove of *tobacciana esoterica*.

I once asked Tom why he didn't publish a companion piece to TPSE focusing solely on snuff, and his reasoning was twofold.

First, he reminded me, snuffing was a tiny niche wrapped inside another niche (smokeless tobacco) inside another niche (alternative tobaccos) in a larger niche (tobacco) that was in danger of being "snuffed out" by anti-tobacco zealotry and legislation based solely on the dangers of the black sheep of the family, the cigarette. He then reminded me of the previous four decades of erratic publishing of TPSE, an unenviable task that he would no doubt not which to duplicate with a sister title. "I thought about it, but there's no way in hell it would work," he once said.

HEDGES

L260 SNUFF

Reg Office
P O Box 71
1205, Stratford Road,
Birmingham, B28 9AG
England

Telephone 021-777-5285
Telex 36125 Perma G
Company Reg. No 678136 ENGLAND

Your Ref   Our Ref   DGW/MR   Date 1st November, 1983.

Mr. Tom Dunn,
The Pipe Smokers Ephereris,
20-37 120th Street,
College Point,
New York 11356,
United States of America.

Dear Mr. Dunn,

You probably are aware that Hedges Snuff is a very good seller in America and it
may interest you to have some of the background of why it is so popular in the
United Kingdom where we are the brand leader.

It is used by the majority of coalminers in the United Kingdom and also business
executives as well as professional people such as accountants and lawyers. It
has a low risk element.

Hedges L260 Snuff was founded over one hundred years ago and is a registered
prescription under L260 in the Pharmacists Prescription Book and was prescribed
for people suffering from hayfever, asthma, colds, bad heads, too much drink etc.
and is still used for these purposes in the United Kingdom. It has tremendous
possibilities and is a well sought after product in the United Kingdom for the
young as well as the middle aged and retired gentle folk. I think your reports
should consider the value of Hedges L260 Snuff and for your help and guidance I
am forwarding you one of our brochures together with a 'Make Friends with Snuff'
leaflet and window stickers which are used extensively in the United Kingdom.

I trust you find the foregoing of interest and will publish some information on
Hedges L260 Snuff.

I send you best regards from the United Kingdom.

Yours sincerely,

M Riley

D.G. Whatley
Managing Director

Dictated by Mr. Whatley and signed in his absence by Mrs. M. Riley Secretary.

Directors: D. G. Whatley (Managing), W. Pettinger, M. J. Cassidy

13th November, 1983

D. G. Whatley, Esq.
Managing Director
HEDGES SNUBB
P.O. Box 71
1205, Stratford Road,
Birmingham, B28 9AG - ENGLAND

Dear Mr. Whatley,

My thanks for your welcome missive and enclosures sent on 1st November.

I am pleased to have this information, which I shall share with my readers

in the next issue of the Ephemeris, due out sometime early, 1984.

Meanwhile, with every good wish for the Holiday Season, I am,

Yours faithfully,

But his archives show that as early as 1965, Tom had kicked around the idea of publishing more material devoted to snuff. While the international feedback was resoundingly in favor of such an endeavor, the lukewarm response here in the US probably reinforced his opinion that snuffing was not as widespread a hobby enough to warrant its own publication. He was, however, a founding member of the Mürren Snuff Club, a Swiss-based international committee devoted to the practice of snuff-taking. It was the first modern international community of its kind, and it is still active today.

But what was I to do with these archives? I originally planned on starting a website to house all the information, but I could never settle on a format for the site that would allow it to be navigated easily enough to find whatever article one searched for. I decided to wait.

When looking for a tobacco magazine to read at the dentist's office one day, I stumbled upon the inspiration for our book, and then it hit me: *this* was the format that the archives needed to be published in. The printed word was just as timeless as the information I wanted to share, and to do it in a regularly printed periodical meant that the stockpile of data could grow ever larger. I felt the whole time that Tom's spirit was urging me on, guiding me in our project. When Mick and I realized that this thing was indeed going to happen, we had to settle on a title. For two days and nights I went back and forth with literally dozens of names, but none of them seemed quite right.

"Snuff Magazine"? No, too modern. Might attract sickos thinking we have some sort of snuff film fetish. In the wake of PACT and The Tobacco Control Act a month previous, I already knew that we would garner the attention of certain government agencies, and I didn't want them to think we were serial killers. (Although I hear that misprinting an FDA warning on an ad for smokeless tobacco now carries the same sentence as murdering 70 people.)

"Snuff Taker's *Gazette? Journal? Atlas? Almanac*?" Hmm, getting warmer. Those names were too... vanilla. I wanted something a little different. Something strange. Something out of left field that really made you take notice.

I always liked that various mags like *Fangoria, Cinemafantastique, Electric Velocipede* and (cough) *Lady Churchill's Rosebud Wristlet* had titles that were sort of off-putting at first glance, but etched itself into the brain once the reader familiarized himself with the publication. A title like "*Cemetery Dance*" makes you do a double take at first, but how could you ever forget such a great name?

It was then that I heard Tom Dunn's voice in my head (at least, what I imagine Tom sounded like. Having never heard him speak, it sounded sort of like a cross between John Wayne and Fred Gwynne). "The Snuff Taker's Ephemeris" was so perfect, I couldn't believe I hadn't thought of it already. It would be a fitting title for the snuff magazine that I think Tom always wanted to do, but never had the chance. A way to honor Tom's memory on the cover of every issue. Most importantly, "The Ephemeris" would evoke the spirit of Tom's seminal work, and it would give us a benchmark of high quality to live up to with each subsequent volume.

If you've never had the opportunity to read a back issue of *The Pipe Smoker's Ephemeris*, you should take it upon yourself to track one down. It is still the best magazine ever made on the subject of tobacco. We hope that our book will be remembered as the second best.

STE

Building The First Issue

RW Hubbard

From conception to design to first printing, STE Volume One took approximately four months to materialize. Most of this period is a blur to me and everyone else involved in the design. Originally we planned on the STE being a full sized, glossy 8.5 x 11 squarebound magazine to run about 80 pages. (This first cover mock-up can be seen on page 4 of this edition.) After receiving about twelve different printing estimates, we realized that the only way we could publish it at this size and keep a 10.00 cover price was if the entire magazine, including covers, was roughly 14 pages long. In black and white, it could have been about 40 pages. So we had to downsize.

We next looked into doing a short, wide book, 7.25 inches wide and 8.5 inches tall. (Think of a piece of legal-sized paper folded in half.) Unfortunately at this size the magazine would have had to be squarebound (glued down the spine like a book as opposed to being stapled three times like a magazine) which was more expensive, and we would have had to drop the page count considerably.

Below is my original front cover mock-up for this aborted "square" size:

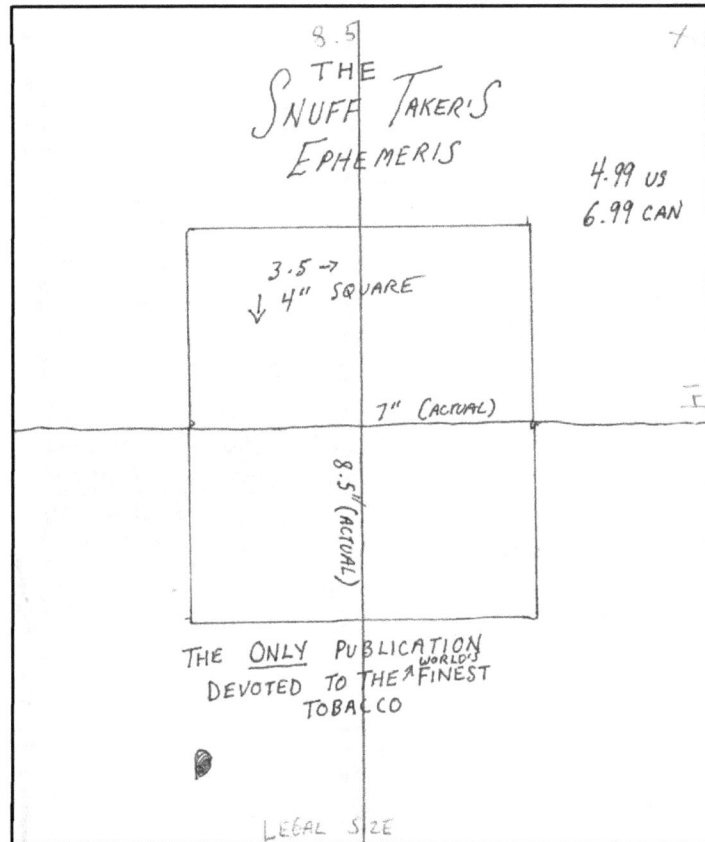

Many of the articles that were "in the can" were also mocked up for this format. Here you can see Jim Walter's "Legal Weed" essay in rough form. (It was later published in our second volume).

K2, or Spice as it is seen here in one of its many brands.

suffered a severe panic attack, Rozga then got up and started walking away from the group. His friends asked him where he was going, and Rozga answered "hell". He then went home and shot himself in the head.

Having just graduated high school and getting ready to prepare for college, it's possible that Rozga may have been under undue stress, and the mother of one of his friends states that Rozga had talked to her about suicide at least once. However, the majority of his friends and friends blame the K2 drug for his suicide, stating that Rozga was neither depressed nor suicidal before smoking K2. Committing suicide was "completely, utterly out of character for him. He was the happiest, most upbeat kid you could meet," claims his mother.

Regardless of whether or not K2 is to blame for Mike Rozga's death, the fact remains that in 80% of the country, K2 is readily available both locally and over the internet. Here in Dallas, you can find K2 and its variants in

pretty much any flea market, head shop, and independent convenience store or gas station in plain sight. Most times it's sitting right next to the register, or next to the lighters or rolling paper displays. None of the shopkeepers interviewed knew exactly where it came from, only that it was manufactured in China. They order it out of catalogs that specialize in "tobacco pipe" culture- that is, poorly printed and misspelled magazines that feature half-naked models wearing pot leaf bandannas on the cover. Inside you can find cannabis-themed attire as well as bongs, stash boxes, lighters, grinders, rolling papers, "one hitters", magical potions that cleanse the urine in preparation for a drug test, "whippets", and plastic snuff rockets. (I'm *positive* that the majority of people buying those snuff bullets are actually using them for good ole Railroad Mills Maccoboy, right?)

K2 sells for roughly the same price as genuine marijuana, though the price seems to be on the rise due to the increased threat of criminalization. This has lead to theft rings that specialize in breaking into head shops and robbing their supply of K2, to be sold back on the street by local drug dealers. Fayetteville, NC police report that one such gang has netted approximately ten thousand dollars worth of K2 by robbing local merchants, and are selling it back on the streets at a much lower cost than the shops sell it for.

There is even a burgeoning *fake* "fake weed" industry. Counterfeit K2 made up of catnip or oregano is being sold by less scrupulous vendors, or those that have no idea that they're not selling the genuine article. These too come out of China, but all of the specimens I came

across were said to have originated in Mexico. The fake K2 is easily distinguishable by the scent it gives off while being smoked- a cross between burning carpet and melting plastic. (*Real* K2 smells sort of like spicy potpourri in the bag, and while being smoked gives off a slightly pungent smell reminiscent of genuine marijuana.)

So, while kids across the country are easily purchasing a cheap, legal, more potent and possibly more dangerous drug than the old standby mary jane, our lawmakers are concentrating on stamping out the *real* menace- flavored tobacco.

Adult tobacco users have suffered all manner of indignation this past year. Between the PACT Act, the FDA takeover of the tobacco industry, SCHIP tax increases heaped upon other tax increases, and attempted bans on reduced harm tobacco products nationwide, it seems that there is a strange double standard in place for the benefit of "the children".

How many children order tobacco online? Well, as far as the government is aware, **none**. Unable to produce a study that shows an epidemic number of minors ordering tobacco products online, the people behind the PACT Act simply cite *potential* numbers. Wait a minute- an unconstitutional and dangerous (in its ramifications) federal mandate was passed on basis of *imaginary statistics*?!?!?

How about the very real statistics that show that minors who purchase K2 do most of their shopping online for it? Yet, tobacco gets the blame for all of the nation's ills.

The FDA now controls the tobacco industry in North America. On the long lists of things that they have done to "save the children", we

have such laugh...
as larger warn...
descriptions on...
color blind if y...
distinguishes a...
its "light" and...
color of the pac...
stomping regul...

Whether you ar...
you have to ad...
are stupid. The...
only tax colle...
make it impo...
snus. "Quit or...
And we're don...

Meanwhile, in ...
kid can walk in...
a dime bag of...
the street with...
had to quit smo...
though, becau...
was the root of...

I'm sure with...
municipalities...
outlawed K2 ...
even suggestin...
criminalize it, ...
the time bein...
world. A world...
in the state o...
package of Ca...
has to settle fo...
Acapulco.

I can't speak f...
catch my kid w...

Handwritten margin notes: "GREY LINE", "6.13", "GUTTER - 0.25", "8.4"

We finally realized that we were going to be a large digest size. This compromise didn't make me very happy, but at least we could run 80 full-color pages and keep the glossy paper.

After settling on a printer (a Moroccan gentleman of limited English), he grabbed a standard 8.5x11 piece of paper and folded it in half. "This be the only way you afford to do," he said. My (lack of) enthusiasm can be witnessed in the doodles I made while sitting in his office waiting on a quote. The top pic is the inside and outside of the front and back "covers" and the bottom pic is my two page interior "layout." No, I'm not proud of this in the least.

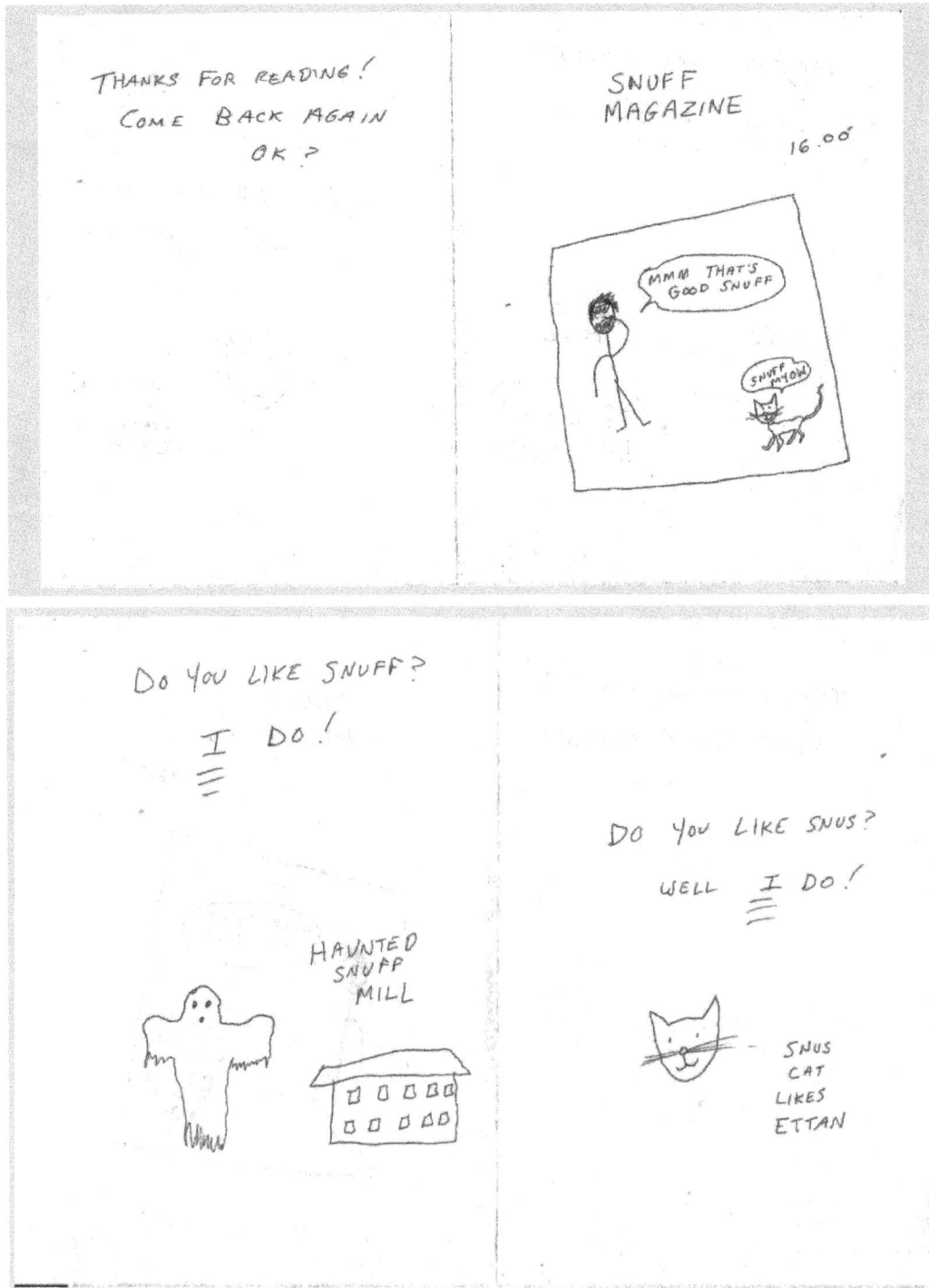

So now the magazine was actually scheduled to print. But we still didn't have a cover. I ran home and whipped up the inside and outside cover and faxed it to everyone for their opinion. It was good, but it needed something for the back, which I finished about 5:00 AM so I could rush it to the printer, who needed it by 7 AM.

THE
SNUFF
TAKER'S
EPHEMERIS

5.51 USA
6.62 CAN
7.28 EUR

DeVOE'S

EXTRA QUALITY

EAGLE MILLS
SCOTCH SNUFF

DEVOE'S EXTRA QUALITY COSTS
YOU LESS TO USE, BECAUSE ITS
QUALITY MAKES IT LAST SO LONG.
JUDGE FOR YOURSELF.
DEVOE SNUFF COMPANY, NASHVILLE, TENN.

Premiere Issue

VOLUME ONE
FALL 2010

On the cover: DeVoe's Eagle Mills Snuff

DeVoe's Eagle Mills Snuff was chosen to adorn our inaugural issue because it's truly an international product that represented all major styles of snuff.

The Eagle Mills were built in Spottswood, NJ by French Huguenot Isaac DeVoe (nee, *Deveaux*) somewhere around 1835. Isaac began by milling popular brands of French snuff of the time, such as Paris *Rapé* (later, *Rappee*) and Carrotte *Parfume*.

While the brands initially sold well, in order to penetrate the lucrative Midwestern snuff market, DeVoe hired mill hands from all over the world to make regional snuffs. Soon he had Scots-Irish, Scandinavian, Bavarian and Polish snuffmakers turning out recipes for dozens of different DeVoe brands.

In addition to the French blends, there was Lundy Foot (also sold as Irish High Toast and Irish Blackguard), Plain Scotch, Sweet Scotch, Rose Maccoboy (also sold as Polish and Holland snuff), Eagle Snus (also sold as Salted Scotch, Swedish, and Eagle Mills [Swedish] Chewing Snuff), German; and all of the other major styles of the era: SP, Medicated, Brunswick (Black Rappee), Burgundy and Göteborg Rappee.

Around the turn of the century, DeVoe (like pretty much every single tobacco maker in the county found itself under the umbrella of the American Tobacco Company, which later devolved into the American Snuff Company. In 1911, after the American trust was dissolved, DeVoe was taken by Weyman-Bruton (makers of Copenhagen and Bruton Snuff). In 1922, Weyman-Bruton became the United States Tobacco Company.

Today, the only remainder of the DeVoe snuff legacy is DeVoe Sweet Snuff, which can still be found on some store shelves, although Altria has officially de-listed it from their product catalog. It remains to be seen if the DeVoe brand has truly met its fate...

•TE

Bill Lee has just spent the last seventy-two hours underground.

He wasn't down there for fun. He was down there earning a living, the only way he knows how. And tonight, he's going to do it all over again.

Because Bill is a coal miner. And his only companion twelve miles below the earth is his snuffbox. And it's the only thing waiting for him when he gets home.

Bill Lee is a snuff taker. The Ephemeris is his magazine.

Reserve your copy of The Snuff Taker's Ephemeris today at www.snuffmagazine.org.

80 CLASS A
PAGES

5.52 USA
6.64 CAN
7.28 EUR

THE SNUFF TAKER'S EPHEMERIS

Don't look for premiums or coupons, as the value of the information contained within THE EPHEMERIS prohibits the use of them.

MANUFACTURED BY
LUCIEN PUBLISHING CO.
FAYETTEVILLE, NC 28390 USA

CHOICE
QUALITY
ARTICLES

DEVOE'S EXTRA QUALITY COSTS YOU LESS TO USE, BECAUSE ITS QUALITY MAKES IT LAST SO LONG. *JUDGE FOR YOURSELF.* DEVOE SNUFF COMPANY, NASHVILLE, TENN.

Premiere Issue

VOLUME ONE
FALL 2010

The damned centerfold from our first printing. For some reason, the printers thought it would be a good idea to print this page upside down, resulting in another 48 hours worth of work on our end. Going through each copy, I would remove the original staples with a staple puller and flat-tipped screwdriver, flip the page over, and my wife would re-staple the spine. What fun that was!

Ye Olde Haunted Snuff Mill?

Strange occurrences rumored to transpire at abandoned New Jersey snuff factory

- Cedar Grove's major claim to fame is that the crossword puzzle was invented there in 1913

The Ephemeris received a letter from a Mrs. G. Hoffman of Old Bridge, NJ, shortly before going to press. We present the letter here in its entirety; its interpretation rests solely in the minds of our readers.

Dear Mr. Hubbard,

Perhaps you can help me with something that's been bugging me for the last sixty odd years!

When I was a little girl my family lived in Cedar Grove, NJ and on the east side of town there was this really old snuff mill there. This was back in the depression times, thirties and forties, and we children didn't have much to do in those days except play around.

Well, this old mill was abandoned for God knows how long, and all of the kids would dare each other to go in the mill or to spend the night in there. It was supposed to be haunted by the ghost of the man that built it, and there was a story going around that he had killed his family and burned down the plant with himself inside of it.

Supposedly, at night you could see his ghost inside of the mill looking out of the window, and rumor had it that there were several kids that went in the mill and

If anyone out there has any information regarding the Cedar Grove Snuff Mill, please drop us a line at the address listed at the end of the article.

Our very first outside ad. I had this printed up half-poster size and distributed throughout the Raleigh-Durham area, where we became an instant hit with college bookstore hipsters. We also ran the ad in a half a dozen fanzines which attracted curious readers. (Notice that the ad makes no mention whatsoever of tobacco, aside from the word "snuff" in the title). We later dusted this ad off and slightly altered it, and it ran in Volume IV.

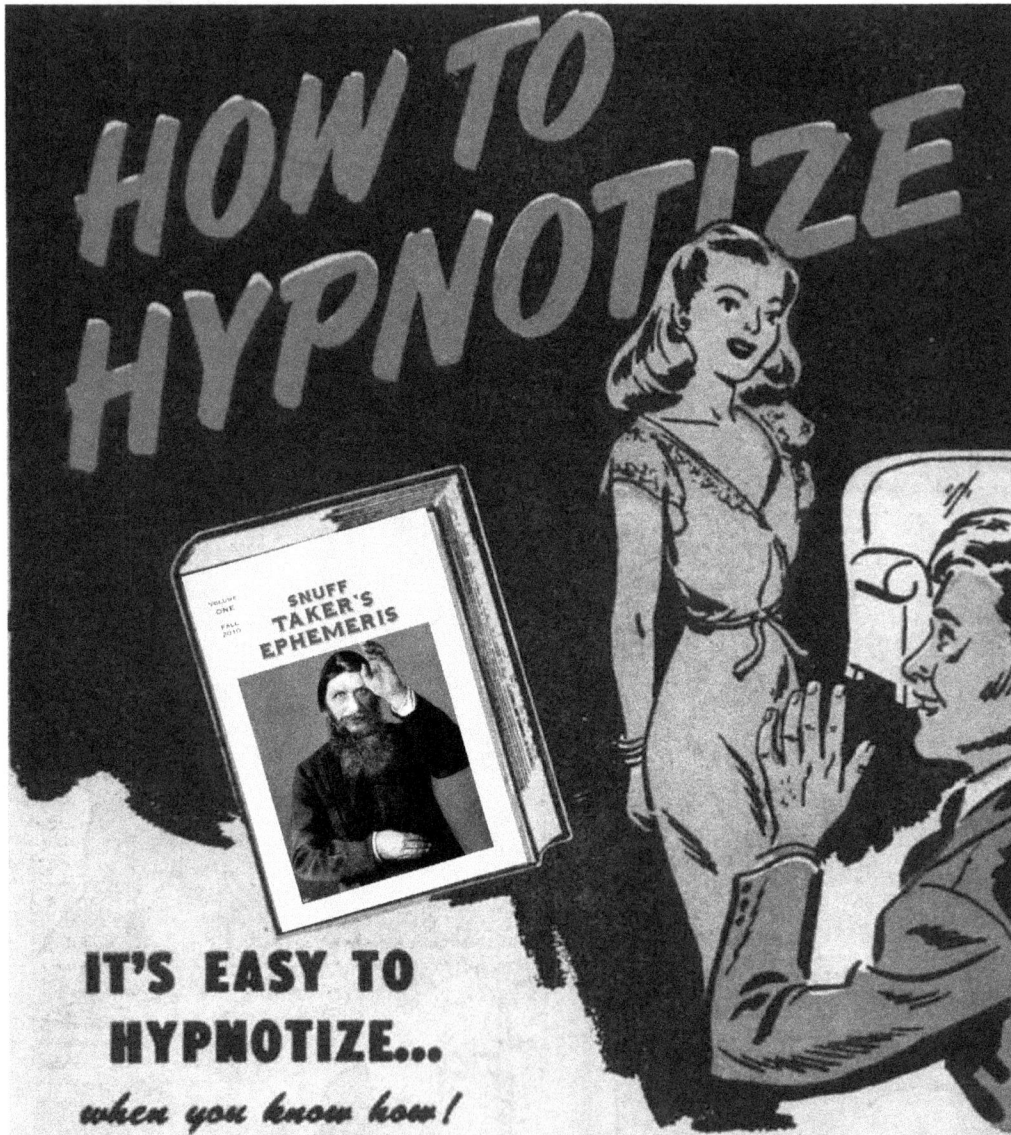

And finally, just for fun. Shortly after Volume One shipped I got a call from an Indian telemarketer trying to sell me stock photos of Lady Gaga to use for the magazine. While annoyed at the time, I later thought it would be an excellent concept.

THE
SNUFF TAKER'S
EPHEMERIS

3.77 USA
212.48 CAN

EPHEMERIS EXCLUSIVE:
LADY GAGA EATS AN ENTIRE CAN OF SQUARE SNUFF WHILE PRETENDING TO BE A ROBOT

PICS INSIDE!

VOLUME TWO   FEB. 2011

We hope you enjoyed this short foray into our genesis. It gave us a chance to dust off some old files that may otherwise have never seen the light of day. As always, thanks for the support the last couple of years and we hope you'll stick around for Volume 100.

STE

FRANZ VON STUCK

A huge influence on the overall look and style of *The Snuff Taker's Ephemeris* comes directly from the legendary Bavarian painter Franz von Stuck (1863-1928).

von Stuck was a dedicated snuffer, and was said to consume up to a pound a day. At times he even mixed snuff into some of his paint in order to give it a unique texture.

Franz von Stuck's works are noted for combining sheer beauty with often disturbing imagery. His paintings were considered very provocative for the time and were sometimes banned from exhibition for their unbridled portrayal of lust and sensuality.

von Stuck was also a sculptor, and this may have been the reason that contemporary critics labeled him a Symbolist painter due his mythical statue-esque painted forms. von Stuck, however, considered himself a student of the Art Nouveau movement. His popularity would fade during the first World War and his work was largely forgotten until the 1960's and 70's, when artists like Andy Warhol and H.R. Giger cited him as one of their primary influences.

We have chosen to adorn the covers of our Master Series reprints with four of von Stuck's best known paintings. This issue we are featuring "Kiss of the Sphinx" (1895). For further exploration, we recommend Eva Mendgen's out of print but indispensable *von Stuck* (Taschen, 1994).

STE®

www.ingramcontent.com/pod-product-compliance
Lightning Source LLC
Chambersburg PA
CBHW081543040426
42448CB00015B/3202